Comfort food is a good thing—whether you're cooking it or unabashedly enjoying it. In her fourth cookbook, Mary Berg, award-winning television host and bestselling author, shares the recipes that bring her and her loved ones the most comfort. If you're looking for a feast to mark a celebratory occasion, a meal to pull on your nostalgic heartstrings, or a dish that will hit the spot when you're feeling a little off, you can count on Mary to help you find the perfect recipe.

- **FIRST THINGS FIRST** Start your morning with a smile, with Bananas Foster Pancakes or Smoked Salmon & Spinach Quiche.
- **A TOAST TO SOUP** Try the Seared Mushroom Ricotta Toast alongside the Chive & Mushroom Soup for the ultimate warming meal.
- **SNACK TOWN** Looking for sour? Try the Pickle Dip. Want something spicy? Try the Crispy Baked Buffalo Wings with Blue Cheese Ranch.
- **STARCH CITY** Population: bread and potatoes! Find Focaccia 4 Ways and the Crispiest Roast Potatoes.
- **VEGGIN' OUT** Think green, with Shredded Kale Salad with Crispies or Caesar Roasted Veg, or check out Nachos for Dinner, a.k.a. a bed of roasted veggies topped with all your favorite nacho fixings.
- **PASTA PLEASE** Cheesy, saucy, stuffed, or baked, the pasta-bilities are endless. Pick from Shorty Carbonara, Spicy Gnocchi alla Vodka, or Mac & Cheese 5 Ways.
- **GONE FISHIN'** Enjoy flavor-packed fish in a flash, with Roasted Salmon 4 Ways or Get-Ahead Fish & Chips.
- **MEATY MORSELS** Go for a low-and-slow Pork Ragu, or indulge in a familiar favorite like Classic BBQ'd Chicken.
- **LI'L SWEETIES** Enjoy PB&J Bars for a taste of childhood, or a light and refreshing Lemon Posset.

Mary loves the go-to classic dishes—or what she calls "comfort-core" recipes, like mac and cheese, biscuits, and meatballs—so she's given them some extra attention, with specially designed sections and multiple flavor variations. You're not getting just one biscuit recipe, you're getting three; you're not getting just one mac and cheese recipe, you're getting five!

In *Mary's Comfort Classics*, there are recipes full of golden-brown deliciousness, vegetable-forward surprises, and starchy, cheesy delights. These are recipes that will become the kitchen equivalents of your favorite sweaters: comforting classics you'll reach for time and time again.

Mary's Comfort Classics

FOOD TO FILL YOUR PLATE

Mary Berg

appetite
by RANDOM HOUSE

Library and Archives Canada Cataloguing in Publication is available upon request.

ISBN: 9780525611967
eBook ISBN: 9780525611974

Photography by Kyla Zanardi
Food styling by Mary Berg and Michelle Lucas Larving
Prop styling by Cailen Speers
Book and cover design by Sid Watson
Typeset by Daniella Zanchetta
Printed in China

The authorized representative in the EU for product safety and compliance is Penguin Random House Ireland, Morrison Chambers, 32 Nassau Street, Dublin, D02 YH68, Ireland, https://eu-contact.penguin.ie

Published in Canada by Appetite by Random House®,
a division of Penguin Random House Canada Limited.
320 Front Street West, Suite 1400
Toronto, Ontario, M5V 3B6, Canada
penguinrandomhouse.ca

10 9 8 7 6 5 4 3 2 1

appetite by RANDOM HOUSE | Penguin Random House Canada

For my guy, Aaron. Thanks for letting me steal (and spill on) all your favorite sweatshirts.

Contents

Veggin' Out

Pasta Please

Gone Fishin'

Meaty Morsels

Li'l Sweeties

Food Is Comfort

It will come as a surprise to exactly no one to hear that the biggest, most consistent comfort in my life is food. Of course, digging into a favorite dish would fill anyone with joy, but I've always found solace in everything around food—not just the eating. From daydreaming about flavors, meal planning, list writing, and grocery shopping to chopping, grating, slicing, and measuring ingredients before bringing them together to make something delicious, every single step involved in getting food on the table is a complete thrill to me. So it's probably a no-brainer that I ended up writing recipes for a living, right?

Not so much.

While I gleefully made my way into the kitchen as soon as I was old enough to hold a wooden spoon, I never thought I would end up here. When I was younger, I got the well-meaning advice not to make my passion my work. This was offered to me by a disenchanted creative, and I can see where they were coming from. A thing they had loved doing no longer fed their soul the way it once had. I let that fear take root for a while, but happily I got over it!

That said, I wouldn't call my move into the world of food TV and recipe writing a cakewalk. Putting myself in the anything-but-comfortable situation of a cooking competition show did not do wonders for the old anxiety brain I've got rattling around up here. Even as I moved into classic cooking shows like *Mary's Kitchen Crush* and *Mary Makes It Easy*, the cameras would start rolling and I'd suddenly feel like I had completely forgotten everything I knew about food. But then I'd find myself in my happy place: near a stove with nothing to do but simply cook.

Whether I'm cooking for work or pleasure, I've found that the kitchen is one of the few places where I have always felt comfortable coloring outside the lines. Burnt the onions? Just add a splash of water and no one will notice. Overcooked the chicken? That's what sauce is for! Cake's dipping in the middle? More room for whipped cream, baby! That freedom, that devil-may-care attitude, is at odds with my very type A personality, so it gives me a break from being the pragmatic, orderly gal that I am in most other areas in my life.

Comfort is having someone in your corner.

My thinking is that no matter how your day goes, feeding yourself is a huge accomplishment. Sure, some days that might look like a bowl of cereal eaten over the sink, or crackers and cheese scarfed down in front of your open fridge, but that is OK. On other days, you get to celebrate in the quiet joy of creating something delicious for yourself and those you love. This book, I hope, is one that you'll reach for on either of those kinds of days—after all, every day deserves a bit of comfort.

Now, the definition of comfort food is a tricky one. There are the obvious players that we all immediately think of, like deep-fried snacks and creamy desserts, but I believe that comfort food goes deeper than that. Comfort comes sometimes from nostalgia and sometimes from indulgence, but the underlying thread connecting it all is finding pleasure in the small things.

For me, the kitchen is the perfect place to do just that. Sure, food can easily be a means to an end—you're hungry, so you eat—but every single time you dig into something, you get the opportunity to enjoy. There is comfort in creating and cooking, there is comfort in the moment of rest that goes hand in hand with eating, and there is comfort in unabashedly enjoying food.

From breakfast and snacks to mains and desserts, you'll find recipes to suit every mood as you cook your way through these pages. There are dishes that pull on those nostalgic heartstrings or are perfect for those times when some jabroni's being a jabroni. There are recipes full of golden-brown deliciousness and starchy, cheesy delights. No matter your vibe, these recipes are designed to bring comfort in how simple they are to get on your table and how they manage to nourish both stomachs and souls alike.

Throughout the book, I've included a few "comfort-core" recipes for those dishes that play on repeat in my house. From breakfast bread puddings and other bready things to mac and cheese and meatballs, these variations will help keep your plate fresh while maintaining that sense of craveable familiarity.

Like all my books, this book is a love letter to what I love to cook and eat—dishes that feed not only the bellies but also the hearts of the people I love. In my house, food is comfort. Hopefully each recipe you find here will be to your kitchen and table what your favorite sweatshirt is to your wardrobe: a welcoming staple you reach for again and again.

Now, break out your soft pants and let's get cozy!

Some Thoughts on Ingredients

This has always been one of my favorite parts of any cookbook—the unassuming section where the author casually drops tidbits of information about their own personal kitchen as well as little kernels of knowledge that they've picked up along the way.

As this book is all about comfort and ease, I've written recipes that are easily customizable to your own whims and fancies. If you are a maverick in the kitchen who needs no approval, you do you, but for those among us who are strict recipe followers, here is a peek into my pantry and a few helpful notes on substitutions. After all, sometimes comfort means not having to run to the store.

SEASONINGS

Salt really is a cook's best friend. It obviously seasons everything it touches, but it also enhances flavors by drawing out moisture during the cooking process. By adding salt at every step, you are effectively concentrating the flavor of each ingredient, which leads to the tastiest results. And salt isn't just important for savory foods—it acts as the perfect foil to all things sweet too.

My go-to salt for both cooking and baking is kosher salt, with Diamond Crystal being my brand of choice. If you prefer to use sea salt in your kitchen, I suggest using slightly less than what is called for in the recipes, as sea salt is finer and brinier than kosher and will give whatever you add it to a saltier flavor.

I am currently obsessed with bouillon, which is a relatively new staple in my household. Having a tin of the powdered stuff on hand makes it a breeze to add extra flavor to roasted vegetables, and a jar of Better Than Bouillon seasoning paste in my fridge door has saved countless half-used containers of store-bought broth from going down the drain. But yes, bouillon, either cubed or paste, is quite salty, so if you're using it, just pull back a bit on the salt in the recipe as a whole.

As for my spice cupboard, other than pepper and nutmeg, I typically buy my spices pre-ground. They are quick and easy to use, and as long as they haven't been languishing on the shelf for more than 3 years, they bring a ton of flavor. You'll see throughout the book that I reach for the spice cupboard a lot. While I'm always stocked with a few herb blends, cumin, smoked paprika, coriander, turmeric, garlic powder, onion powder, chili powder, cayenne, and crushed red pepper flakes, you can swap like for like if you're missing something. For instance, if I'm looking for something smoky but I'm out of smoked paprika, I'll reach for cumin and chili powder. If I'm out of cayenne, crushed red pepper flakes will do. And if I'm out of Italian seasoning, I just use whatever dried herbs I have hanging around.

FATS

Whether making something savory or sweet, use whatever butter you have on hand—that is, unless you're browning it. Unsalted butter is best for brown butter because you don't have to worry about overconcentrating the salt as you simmer it down.

For oils, my pantry staples are a tasty yet cost-effective extra virgin olive oil for cooking, a peppery finishing extra virgin olive oil for things like dressings and drizzling, and good old Canadian canola oil for high-heat applications and any recipes that require a neutral-tasting oil. Unless the oil is being used as a main flavor agent in a recipe, you can use any oil you'd like. If canola oil isn't your bag, any neutral oil will do.

DRY GOODS

Being someone who loves to bake, I typically have all-purpose flour and bread flour on hand, but all you really need is all-purpose flour. While bread flour is best for bread, you can substitute it with all-purpose without too noticeable a difference (the bread will be slightly less risen and have less springy chew, but it will still be delicious).

As you get into the baking recipes, granulated sugar is a must and brown sugar is a nice-to-have. If you don't have brown sugar on hand or it's turned into a rock-solid brick, reach into the back of your pantry for that carton of molasses you bought last Christmas. Making your own fresh brown sugar is as easy as blitzing 1 cup of granulated sugar with 1 tablespoon of molasses for light brown sugar or 2 tablespoons for dark brown sugar.

DAIRY

All dairy is full-fat, including cheese, cream cheese, sour cream, and yogurt. Lower-fat varieties tend to be watery and contain stabilizers that don't react well to heat or to mixing. Dollop-able dairy, such as Greek yogurt, sour cream, and skyr, can be used interchangeably unless heated in a sauce—in those cases, stick with what I've recommended for the recipe. For cheeses, if you don't have a specific variety called for, simply pick any cheese you like that has a similar texture and melty-ness.

Those who have watched me cook over the years know that I have a soft spot for something I affectionately call "shaky cheese." For those not in the know, I'm talking about that canister of ground Parmesan cheese that you find in the pasta sauce aisle of your grocery store. Now, I know not everyone shares my adoration of the stuff, so feel free to use ground Parmigiano-Reggiano in its place. In my house, there are only two recipes that *require* shaky cheese (Cheddar Ritz Chicken on page 176 and A Southern Spin on Myra's Mac on page 143), but you do you. When any Parm is mentioned in an ingredient list, make sure you pay attention to whether it is ground or grated, as they mix and melt differently into recipes.

For milk, I'm a 3.25% gal and all recipes have been tested with that, but you can use 2% if that's what your family keeps in the fridge. When a recipe calls for cream, I specify the percentage if it is integral to the success of the dish. If the ingredient list does not specify the percentage, use any cream you have on hand.

As for buttermilk, I feel like I'm the only person in the world who can actually make her way through a whole carton. For everyone other than me, all instances of buttermilk can be substituted with the classic soured milk substitute. Simply add 1 teaspoon of white vinegar, apple cider vinegar, or lemon juice to a measuring cup and top with milk so that it reaches the 1-cup mark. Let it sit for a few minutes and you're good to go.

PRODUCE

Each recipe containing herbs provides a measurement for them, but my advice is to measure with your heart. If you've ever seen me cook on TV, you know that "1 tablespoon of dill" is rarely less than ¼ cup of dill, so who am I to restrain your herb usage? Fresh herbs are a big flavor booster to every dish they grace, and I highly recommend getting into them, but dried will work in a pinch. If you're using dried, use about one-quarter of what's called for in the recipe.

In the world of fresh herbs, there are two main camps: fine and woody. Parsley, cilantro, tarragon, basil, mint, dill, and chives are considered fine herbs, whereas rosemary, oregano, thyme, and sage are woody. As long as you stick within these categories, you can kind of use these herbs interchangeably. Whatever you use will obviously alter the flavor of the dish, but if you like it, go for it.

I'm a big proponent of using what you have. Dark, leafy greens like kale, spinach, chard, and collards are all easily swappable except for in the Greens & Cheese Pasta (page 144) and the Shredded Kale Salad with Crispies (page 108). The same goes for roasting hearty veg. Veg that can take the heat of the oven, like squash, peppers, fennel, onions, yams, potatoes, cauliflower, and broccoli, can all be used in each other's place.

When buying yellow and red onions, go for the bulk bag. The onions not only typically last longer but are also much more affordable and are typically a consistent, smaller size that's perfect for most recipes.

In recipes that call for a red onion, yellow onion, white onion, or shallot, feel free to use those interchangeably. The only note is that shallots are typically about half the size of an onion, so use two shallots in place of one onion or half an onion in place of one shallot.

PROTEINS

Perhaps my most-used substitute in the kitchen is ground meat. I don't know about you, but every week at my local grocery store, one ground meat or another is on sale. Having always loved a bargain, I find the on-sale choice too good to pass up, so I've lately taken to swapping pork for chicken or chicken for beef, to great results.

"FANCY" THINGS

I tend to "Smaug" things in the kitchen and beyond . . . and for those of you who did *not* spend their formative years marching through Middle Earth, that basically means I like to sit on my most treasured items. I keep things around, tucked in the back of cupboards, closets, and drawers, and save them for that perfect moment. The only problem? That's not how life works. 99.9 percent of the things I've squirreled away have either been forgotten or spoiled before I used them, so take it from me, use the vanilla bean in a no-reason cake, glug that snazzy olive oil all over a bowl of pasta on a random Tuesday, and use that "only for the fanciest charcuterie board" jam on your morning toast! You deserve it.

TOMATO TO

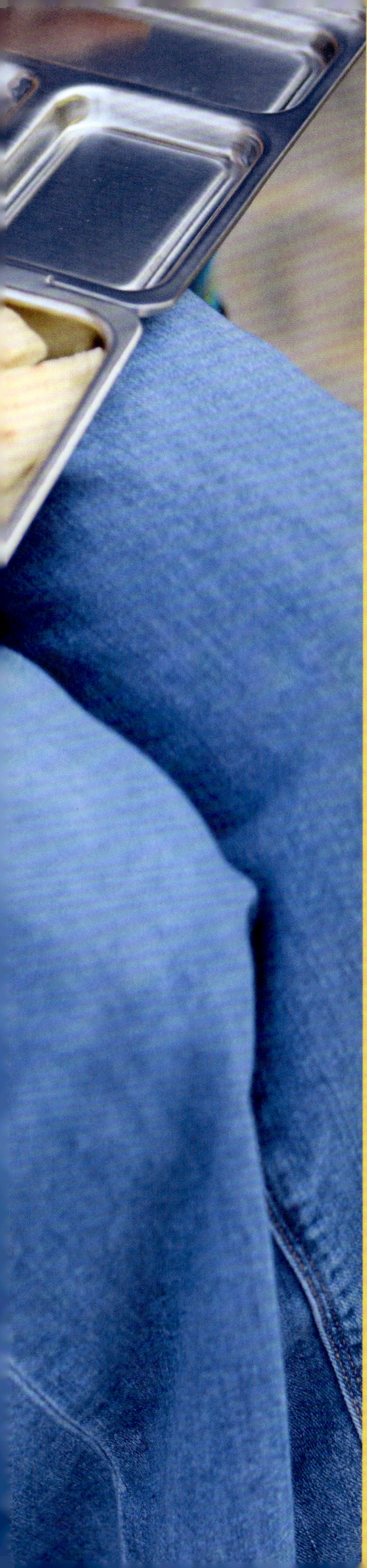

The Why

I've given you a brief overview of ingredients and the way I approach them, but there's another piece of the puzzle that I want to tackle here. With respect to the recipe methods and my writing in general, I think it's helpful to know that I was and always will be a "why" kid (much to the frustration of many adults in my life growing up). If I know *why* I'm being asked to do something, I'll remember to do it next time. This inquisitive process is especially handy in the kitchen, and I try to keep it front of mind when putting together all my recipes.

In addition to the explanations on pages 5 to 8 as to why I use or call for certain ingredients, I've offered tips and tricks within the recipe methods and as little sidenotes throughout this book; hopefully they'll find their way into the Rolodex in your brain, ready to retrieve whenever you're in need. That's why my methods are a bit on the wordy side. But there's no faffing about—I'm just trying to give you the info you need and preemptively answer any questions you might have. I hope that every recipe I write not only helps you cook that particular dish but also gives you the confidence and knowledge to tackle any recipe out there.

First Things First

No matter when you wake up, the first thing you eat should always be delicious. Preferably served with some caffeine and enjoyed in your PJs.

I have a hard-and-fast rule when it comes to raisins. They are fine as is, but as soon as you bake them into something and they start to rehydrate, I cannot abide them. You made your bed, raisin! Stop trying to become a zombie grape! But as with any rule, there are always exceptions. Thanks to the nostalgia factor of warm, toasted cinnamon raisin bread slathered with butter and scattered with a pinch of salt, this is the one instance in which baked raisins are A-OK in my books.

Cinnamon Raisin Soda Bread

MAKES 1 LOAF

- 1 cup raisins
- 4 cups whole wheat flour
- ½ cup oats, rolled, quick-cooking, or instant
- 3 tablespoons sugar
- 2 tablespoons cinnamon, divided
- 1 tablespoon baking powder
- 1 teaspoon baking soda
- ¾ teaspoon kosher salt
- 1¾ cups buttermilk (see note)
- ¼ cup butter, melted

Set a kettle to boil and preheat your oven to 425°F. Line a sheet pan with parchment paper.

Place the raisins in a small bowl and pour in enough boiling water to cover. Set aside for 5 minutes to slightly reconstitute the raisins. Drain the raisins and set them aside.

In a large bowl, whisk the flour, oats, sugar, and 1 tablespoon of cinnamon together. Add the baking powder, baking soda, and salt and stir to combine. In a separate bowl or a glass measuring cup, whisk together the buttermilk and butter. Make a well in the center of the dry ingredients and pour in the buttermilk mixture followed by the drained raisins. Using a wooden spoon, stir until a shaggy dough forms. If needed, add a little more milk or flour until the dough comes together and is not too sticky.

Lightly flour a work surface and turn out the dough. Lightly flatten it and scatter the top with the remaining 1 tablespoon of cinnamon. Gently knead the dough two or three times to form a rough loaf and swirl in the cinnamon, being careful not to overwork it.

Transfer the loaf to the prepared sheet pan. With a large knife, score a deep X across the top of the loaf, making sure to cut about halfway down.

Bake for 20 minutes, then turn down the temperature to 325°F and continue to bake for another 20 to 25 minutes, or until golden brown and the loaf sounds hollow when you tap on the top with your knuckles.

Transfer your loaf to a wire rack and allow it to cool before slicing. Once cool, wrap the loaf and store at room temperature for 3 to 4 days or in the freezer for up to 3 months.

Note: If you don't have buttermilk on hand, you can make an easy substitute by stirring regular milk with a dash of white or apple cider vinegar or lemon juice. You'll want to use a ratio of 1 cup of milk to 1 teaspoon of acid.

In my mind, there is a very clear hierarchy in the world of nuts. Obviously, pistachios and cashews are up there, but the best nut of all is clearly the pecan. Falling toward the bottom of the barrel is, in my personal opinion, the hazelnut. When it's masked with chocolate in that classic Italian breakfast spread, I will say that I am a fan, but why not just switch out that hazelnut for a pecan and make the *ultimate* chocolaty nut butter?

Chocolate Pecan Butter

MAKES ABOUT 2 CUPS

- 4 cups pecans
- 2 oz dark chocolate, melted
- 1 tablespoon cocoa powder
- ½–1 teaspoon flaky sea salt
- Maple syrup or icing sugar, if needed
- 1–2 tablespoons canola oil, if needed

Preheat your oven to 325°F. Spread the pecans on a large sheet pan. Toast for 5 to 7 minutes, or until they smell nutty, being careful not to burn them.

Transfer the hot toasted pecans to the bowl of your food processor fitted with the steel blade. Process until smooth and creamy, 3 to 6 minutes depending on your food processor, scraping down the bowl as needed.

Add the melted chocolate, cocoa powder, and ½ teaspoon of salt and process to combine. Season to taste with more salt. If desired, add a little maple syrup or icing sugar for added sweetness and 1 to 2 tablespoons of oil for a slightly creamier consistency.

Transfer to a resealable container and store at room temperature for up to 1 week or in the fridge for up to 1 month.

Note: This might just be a note to myself, but if you too are a science nerd, you'll appreciate that this spread is a non-Newtonian fluid!

As you flip through these pages, you'll notice a recurring theme. To me, comfort sometimes means having to make fewer decisions in a day, especially during those times when my brain is feeling a bit like a bowl of instant oatmeal. In those instances, the food that graces my table is often an amalgamation of every flavor I want to dig into at that particular moment. I call these "mash-up" recipes, and this is the first of many. With the sweet dessert-y flavors of bananas Foster meeting a classic stack of flapjacks, I can guarantee your day will be off to a great start.

Bananas Foster Pancakes

SERVES 4 TO 6

FOR THE PANCAKES

1¼ cups all-purpose flour

½ cup whole wheat flour (or more all-purpose)

3 tablespoons sugar

2 teaspoons baking powder

1 teaspoon baking soda

¼ teaspoon cinnamon

Pinch freshly grated nutmeg

½ teaspoon kosher salt

1½ cups buttermilk

¼ cup butter, melted

2 eggs

1 teaspoon vanilla extract

Butter or neutral oil, for cooking

FOR THE BANANAS

3 tablespoons butter

¼ cup dark brown sugar, packed

¼ cup maple syrup

¼ teaspoon kosher salt

¼ teaspoon cinnamon

Pinch freshly grated nutmeg

2 tablespoons dark rum, optional

3 bananas (see note)

¼ cup chopped walnuts

Preheat your oven to 200°F and line a sheet pan with a rack.

For the pancakes, in a large bowl, whisk the flours, sugar, baking powder, baking soda, cinnamon, nutmeg, and salt together. In a separate bowl, whisk together the buttermilk, butter, eggs, and vanilla. Add the wet ingredients to the dry and stir just until combined with a few lumps remaining. This should take only a few good stirs. Set the batter aside.

Heat a large cast-iron or nonstick skillet over medium heat. When hot, add a little butter or oil to the pan to melt. Spoon about ¼ cup of batter per pancake into the skillet and cook until bubbles start to appear on top. When the bubbles start to pop and hold their shape around the sides of the pancakes, check the underside. When golden brown, flip and continue to cook for 1 to 2 minutes until cooked through. Transfer the cooked pancakes to the prepared sheet pan and place in the oven to keep warm while you cook the rest of the pancakes.

Once the pancakes are cooked, prepare the bananas. Return the pan to medium heat and add the butter to melt. Stir in the brown sugar, maple syrup, salt, cinnamon, and nutmeg. Add the rum, if using, being careful of flare-ups, and bring to a low boil.

Meanwhile, peel and halve the bananas, then split lengthwise. Add to the pan along with the walnuts. Cook for about 1 minute, or just until the bananas have softened slightly.

Serve the pancakes topped with the bananas Foster.

Note: Use yellow bananas if possible. Green will be a bit too starchy, and bananas with brown spots will break down too quickly.

There are two types of waffle eaters out there: the grid follower and the chaos agent. As is probably evident by everything about me, I am very obviously in the former camp. From crispy golden-brown homemade waffles to the freezer variety, I have always taken them down one row at a time. Perhaps it's my type A personality speaking, but cutting your waffles into strips along the gridline is the correct way to make a perfect dunker for a steaming mug of rich and creamy hot chocolate.

Waffles & Hot Chocolate

SERVES 4

FOR THE WAFFLES

1¼ cups all-purpose flour

½ cup whole wheat flour (or more all-purpose)

3 tablespoons sugar

2 teaspoons baking powder

1 teaspoon baking soda

½ teaspoon kosher salt

1½ cups buttermilk

¼ cup butter, melted

2 eggs

1 teaspoon vanilla extract

Maple syrup, for serving

FOR THE HOT CHOCOLATE

⅓ cup sugar

¼ cup cocoa powder, sifted

1½ oz semisweet or dark chocolate, finely chopped or grated

1 tablespoon chocolate malted milk powder, such as Milo, Ovaltine, or Horlicks

¼ teaspoon kosher salt

5 cups milk

Preheat your oven to 200°F and place a rack-lined sheet pan in the oven.

For the waffles, in a large bowl, whisk the flours, sugar, baking powder, baking soda, and salt to combine. In a separate bowl, whisk together the buttermilk, melted butter, eggs, and vanilla. Add the wet ingredients to the dry and stir just until combined with a few lumps remaining. Set the batter aside while you heat the waffle iron.

Once the waffle iron is hot, grease it well with some butter or nonstick cooking spray. Add about ½ cup of the batter to each waffle well and cook until golden and crisp, 3 to 5 minutes, or until your waffle iron indicates they are ready. Transfer to the rack-lined sheet pan to keep warm while you cook the remaining waffles and prepare the hot chocolate.

For the hot chocolate, in a medium saucepan, whisk together the sugar, cocoa powder, chocolate, chocolate malted milk powder, and salt. Whisk in the milk and heat over low until steamy.

Serve the waffles with syrup and butter, if desired, and a mug of hot chocolate on the side. Freeze leftover waffles for up to 3 months and reheat in the toaster.

Note: Chocolate malted milk powder adds a sweet nuttiness to this recipe. It's often found near the hot chocolate mixes in the grocery store, but if you can't find it, just omit it from the recipe.

Double or triple the hot chocolate recipe, leaving out the milk, for your own homemade instant hot chocolate mix.

I feel like Sunday gets a bit of a bum rap. Sure, it signals the end of the weekend and can often stir up the dreaded Sunday Scaries, but if you're more of a "glass half full" kind of person, it's the perfect day to bop around your house leisurely setting yourself up for the week. I'm calling this recipe a Sunday soother. It's easy to prep on Sunday afternoon to enjoy throughout the week, yet still celebrates the day where things can slow down.

Brown Butter Pear Baked Oatmeal

SERVES 8

¼ cup unsalted butter
1½ cups steel-cut oats
½ cup chopped pecans
¼ cup hemp hearts, optional
3 tablespoons ground flaxseed
1 egg
3½ cups milk
4–6 tablespoons maple syrup
2 teaspoons vanilla extract
2–3 teaspoons cinnamon
1½ teaspoons baking powder
½ teaspoon kosher salt
3 ripe pears, diced

Preheat your oven to 375°F.

In a large cast-iron skillet, melt the butter over medium heat. Cook the butter for 1 to 2 minutes, until lightly browned. Add the oats, pecans, hemp hearts, if using, and ground flaxseed and stir to combine. Toast the mixture in the pan for about 1 minute, until it starts to smell nutty.

Meanwhile, in a large bowl, beat the egg. Stir in the milk, maple syrup, vanilla, cinnamon, baking powder, and salt.

Remove the pan from the heat, stir in the diced pears, and carefully pour in the milk mixture. Transfer the pan to the oven, placing a sheet pan on the rack below in case of any boil-over, and bake for 45 to 50 minutes, or until set.

Serve hot, or allow the oatmeal to cool to room temperature and store in the fridge for up to 5 days for breakfasts throughout the week.

Note: If you don't have a large cast-iron skillet, toast the oat mixture in a sauté pan or skillet and transfer to a greased 9-by-13-inch baking dish to assemble and bake.

Being someone who loves a project in the kitchen, there are few things I shy away from, but butter tarts and croissants remain insurmountable culinary conundrums—the former thanks to the "Butter Tart Lady" at the Gravenhurst Farmers Market in Muskoka, Ontario, and her unbeatable ooey gooey, flaky tarts, and the latter thanks to my own "simply cannot be bothered with all that rolling, resting, and laminating" vibe. By bringing the flavor of sticky, sweet butter tarts together with the flaky richness of store-bought croissants, I've somehow created something just as indulgent as the originals but about 8,000 times easier.

Butter Tart Croissants

MAKES 6

FOR THE SYRUP

½ cup maple syrup
¼ cup bourbon or rye
¼ cup water
⅓ cup raisins, optional
½ teaspoon vanilla extract

FOR THE CROISSANTS

7 oz pecans, divided
6 tablespoons all-purpose flour
¼ teaspoon kosher salt
½ cup butter, room temperature
½ cup icing sugar
1 tablespoon maple syrup
2 eggs
½ teaspoon vanilla extract
6 day-old croissants (see note)
Icing sugar, for serving

Preheat your oven to 350°F and line a sheet pan with parchment paper.

For the syrup, in a small saucepan, combine the maple syrup, bourbon or rye, and water and bring to a simmer over medium-low heat. Add the raisins, if using. Simmer for 2 to 3 minutes to cook off some of the alcohol and slightly plump the raisins, then remove from the heat and stir in the vanilla. Set aside to cool slightly or all the way to room temperature.

Meanwhile, for the croissants, place 5 oz of pecans in a small food processor and pulse into a fine meal. You want the pecans to be the texture of almond flour. Add the flour and salt, pulse to combine, and set aside. In a medium bowl, beat the butter, icing sugar, and maple syrup until light and fluffy, 1 to 2 minutes by hand or about 1 minute if using an electric mixer. Beat in the eggs one at a time, then beat in the vanilla. Add the pecan flour mixture and mix just to combine.

Slice the croissants in half lengthwise. Set the top halves aside and dunk the bottom halves in the syrup. Transfer to the prepared sheet pan and spread about two-thirds of the pecan mixture overtop. If using raisins, use a slotted spoon to remove them from the remaining syrup and scatter overtop.

Dunk the top halves of the croissants in the syrup, then sandwich on top of the bottom halves. Spread the remaining pecan mixture onto the top of each croissant. Finely chop the remaining 2 oz of pecans and scatter overtop.

Bake the croissants for 20 to 25 minutes, or until golden brown and crisp. Allow them to cool slightly or all the way to room temperature before dusting with icing sugar and serving.

Note: No need to splurge on fancy croissants. The ones from the grocery store bakery or, better yet, that sneaky little rack with day-old baked goods work perfectly in this recipe.

Tuscan Breakfast Bread Pudding 31
Green Eggs & Ham Breakfast Bread Pudding 30
Maple Sausage Breakfast Bread Pudding 29

Rocky Road Breakfast Bread Pudding 28

Breakfast Bread Pudding 4 Ways

Nostalgia is clearly a big player in the world of comfort.

When I was growing up, on every Good Friday my church would host a potluck breakfast that I referred to as "Strata-Fest." I looked forward to the buffet of bready casseroles and watered-down juice more than most kids looked forward to that Sunday's Easter egg hunt.

Ever since those Fridays at church, I've been enamored with what can essentially be described as breakfast bread pudding. Savory or sweet, there's nothing quite like an easy make-ahead breakfast to bring people to the table.

Ice cream for breakfast is a bit of a stretch, but hear me out. What about the *flavors* of ice cream for breakfast? Pretty brilliant workaround, hey?

Rocky Road Breakfast Bread Pudding

SERVES 4 TO 6

- Eight 1-inch-thick slices challah, brioche, or other rich egg bread
- ¼ cup dark brown sugar, packed
- 1 tablespoon cocoa powder
- ¼ teaspoon freshly grated nutmeg
- ¼ teaspoon kosher salt
- 6 eggs
- 1½ cups milk
- ¼ cup cream, 10% or higher
- 1½ teaspoons vanilla extract
- 3½ oz semisweet chocolate, chopped
- 1 cup mini marshmallows
- ½ cup chopped walnuts

Lightly grease a 3-quart baking or casserole dish with nonstick cooking spray and set aside. Lay the slices of bread on a baking rack to allow them to get a bit stale while you prepare the custard.

In a large bowl, whisk together the brown sugar, cocoa powder, nutmeg, and salt. Add the eggs, milk, cream, and vanilla and beat to combine. Soak four slices of bread in the custard for about 20 seconds per side, then arrange in the baking dish so that the slices overlap. Scatter half of the chocolate, marshmallows, and walnuts overtop, then soak and layer on the remaining four slices of bread. Carefully pour any remaining custard overtop, then scatter with the remaining chocolate, marshmallows, and walnuts. Lightly spray the dull side of a piece of aluminum foil with nonstick cooking spray and cover the baking dish, greased side down. Transfer the dish to the fridge and let rest for at least 2 hours or up to overnight.

When ready to bake, remove the dish from the fridge and preheat your oven to 375°F. Bake, covered, for 30 minutes, then remove the foil and continue to bake for 20 to 25 minutes, or until golden brown and set in the middle.

Allow the casserole to rest for 5 minutes before serving.

Note: If this feels a bit too indulgent for your breakfast table, pop a scoop of ice cream on there and call it dessert.

From ages one through five, my diet consisted mainly of breakfast meats. Sure, the bacon tray at the Golden Griddle in Pickering, Ontario, never liked to see me coming, but it was sweet little maple breakfast sausages that really had my number.

Maple Sausage Breakfast Bread Pudding

SERVES 4 TO 6

- Eight 1-inch-thick slices country or sourdough bread
- 1 lb ground pork
- 2 garlic cloves, minced
- 1 tablespoon finely chopped fresh sage
- 1½ teaspoons fennel seeds
- ½ teaspoon smoked paprika
- 2 tablespoons + ¼ cup maple syrup, divided
- Kosher salt
- Freshly ground black pepper
- 1 tablespoon butter or olive oil
- 6 eggs
- 1½ cups milk
- ¼ cup cream, 10% or higher
- ¾ cup shredded white cheddar or smoked cheddar

Lightly grease a 3-quart baking or casserole dish with nonstick cooking spray. Lay the slices of bread on a baking rack to allow them to get a bit stale while you prepare the sausage and custard.

In a large bowl, combine the ground pork, garlic, sage, fennel seeds, and paprika. Pour in 2 tablespoons of maple syrup, season with ½ teaspoon of salt and a bit of pepper, and stir to combine. In a large skillet over medium-high heat, heat the butter or oil, then add the pork mixture. Cook, stirring occasionally, until golden and cooked through, 5 to 7 minutes.

In a large bowl, whisk the eggs. Add the milk, cream, and the remaining ¼ cup of maple syrup and season with salt and pepper. Whisk well to combine. Soak four slices of bread in the custard for about 20 seconds per side, then arrange in the baking dish so that the slices overlap. Scatter with half of the sausage and cheese, then soak and layer on the remaining bread. Carefully pour any remaining custard overtop, then scatter with the remaining sausage and cheese. Lightly spray the dull side of a piece of aluminum foil with nonstick cooking spray and cover the baking dish, greased side down. Transfer the dish to the fridge and let rest for at least 2 hours or up to overnight.

When ready to bake, remove the dish from the fridge and preheat your oven to 375°F. Bake for 30 minutes, then remove the foil and continue to bake for 20 to 25 minutes, or until golden brown and set in the middle.

Allow the casserole to rest for 5 minutes before serving.

Note: If you don't want to make your own sausage meat, fry up 10 to 12 premade breakfast sausage links until fully cooked. Chop into bite-sized pieces and scatter into the casserole.

With no questions about boxes, foxes, boats, goats, houses, or mouses, liking this dish is a total given.

Green Eggs & Ham Breakfast Bread Pudding

SERVES 4 TO 6

Eight 1-inch-thick slices country or sourdough bread, cubed or torn
1½ cups cubed deli ham, divided
1½ cups shredded Swiss cheese, divided
1 tablespoon butter
½ yellow onion, diced
Kosher salt
Freshly ground black pepper
2 garlic cloves, minced
1½ cups well-packed chopped kale
2 tablespoons chopped fresh dill
2 tablespoons chopped fresh parsley
2 teaspoons Dijon mustard
1½ cups milk
¼ cup cream, 10% or higher
6 eggs

Lightly grease a 3-quart baking or casserole dish with nonstick cooking spray. Scatter in half of the bread, then top with half of the ham and half of the cheese. Layer on the remaining bread and set aside.

In a medium skillet over medium heat, melt the butter and add the onions. Season with salt and pepper and cook for 5 minutes, or until softened and lightly golden brown. Stir in the garlic and cook for 30 seconds, then add the kale and season with more salt and pepper. Cover and cook for 1 to 2 minutes just to wilt the greens slightly.

Transfer the greens to your blender along with the dill, parsley, and mustard. Add the milk, cream, and eggs, season with salt and pepper, and blitz until smooth. Slowly pour the egg mixture over the bread in the baking dish and scatter over the remaining ham and cheese. Lightly spray the dull side of a piece of aluminum foil with nonstick cooking spray and cover the baking dish, greased side down. Transfer the dish to the fridge and let rest for at least 2 hours or up to overnight.

When ready to bake, remove the dish from the fridge and preheat your oven to 375°F. Bake for 30 minutes, then remove the foil and continue to bake for 20 to 25 minutes, or until golden brown and set in the middle.

Allow the casserole to rest for 5 minutes before serving.

If you're looking for an authentic Tuscan breakfast, please just go ahead and turn the page now because this is definitely not it. It is, however, a dish that I first threw together while staying in the Tuscan hills to use up odds and ends before heading out to the market to restock the fridge and pantry. With birds singing, a cappuccino in hand, and a forkful of this, start your day living la dolce vita.

Tuscan Breakfast Bread Pudding

SERVES 4 TO 6

8 oz cherry tomatoes, halved
Olive oil
Kosher salt
Freshly ground black pepper
Eight 1-inch-thick slices country or sourdough bread, cubed or torn
3½–5 oz smoked mozzarella, diced
6 eggs
1½ cups milk
¼ cup cream, 10% or higher
¾ cup finely grated pecorino Romano
3–4 tablespoons prepared pesto
Crushed red pepper flakes

Place your oven rack in the middle position and turn the broiler to high.

Place the cherry tomatoes in a 3-quart baking or casserole dish, drizzle with some olive oil, and season with salt and pepper. Broil the tomatoes for 6 to 8 minutes, until lightly charred and juicy. Remove the tomatoes from the dish and set aside, then add a little more oil to coat the bottom and sides of the dish. Scatter in half of the bread, then top with half each of the tomatoes and smoked mozzarella. Scatter on the remaining bread followed by the remaining tomatoes and smoked mozzarella. Set aside.

In a large bowl, whisk the eggs. Add the milk, cream, pecorino Romano, and pesto, and season with red pepper flakes, salt, and pepper. Whisk well to combine. Slowly pour the egg mixture over the bread in the baking dish. Lightly spray the dull side of a piece of aluminum foil with nonstick cooking spray and cover the dish, greased side down. Transfer the dish to the fridge and let rest for at least 2 hours or up to overnight.

When ready to bake, remove the dish from the fridge and preheat your oven to 375°F. Bake for 30 minutes, then remove the foil and continue to bake for 20 to 25 minutes, or until golden brown and set in the middle.

Allow the casserole to rest for 5 minutes before serving.

Nothing is more stressful in the kitchen than overnight guests. The night before, you've already planned, prepped, and made dinner, but that offer of a warm bed and random new toothbrush from your last visit to the dentist has come back to haunt you because I guess you need to make breakfast now too?!

While I have a few last-minute-guest breakfasts up my sleeve, this quiche is a total show-stopper. It's easy enough to throw together in the morning (if you remember to toss some frozen spinach and phyllo into your fridge to thaw overnight), or it's a great make-ahead for the planners among us.

Smoked Salmon & Spinach Quiche

SERVES 8

7 oz frozen spinach
10 sheets frozen phyllo
2 tablespoons olive oil
1 yellow onion, finely diced
Kosher salt
Freshly ground black pepper
2 garlic cloves, minced
3 tablespoons finely chopped fresh dill
3 tablespoons finely chopped fresh parsley
½ teaspoon crushed red pepper flakes
Pinch freshly grated nutmeg
1 lemon, zested and juiced, divided
5–7 oz hot- or cold-smoked salmon
5 eggs
1 cup milk or cream
⅓ cup butter, melted
3½ oz goat cheese or feta, crumbled

The night before you plan on making the quiche, place the frozen spinach and phyllo in the fridge to thaw overnight or for up to 1 day.

The next morning, preheat your oven to 350°F.

For the filling, heat the oil in a medium skillet over medium heat. Add the onions, season with salt and pepper, and cook until softened and lightly golden brown, about 5 minutes. Add the garlic and cook for 1 minute, stirring often, then remove the pan from the heat and stir in the dill, parsley, red pepper flakes, nutmeg, and lemon zest. Set this mixture aside to cool slightly.

Drain the spinach through a strainer lined with a clean kitchen towel or a few layers of sturdy paper towel. Gather the spinach in the towel and firmly squeeze out as much of the water as possible. Transfer the spinach to the pan of onions and add the lemon juice. If using hot-smoked salmon, flake it into the pan. If using cold-smoked salmon, roughly chop it and add it to the pan.

In a large bowl, beat the eggs with the milk or cream, then add the spinach mixture and stir well to combine. Set aside.

Retrieve the phyllo from the fridge, unroll it, and cover with a clean kitchen towel to keep it from drying out. Place a 9-inch springform pan on a rimmed sheet pan and brush the bottom and sides lightly with melted butter. Lay out one sheet of phyllo, brush it with butter, and transfer it to the prepared pan. There is no need to be extra careful here—the phyllo might tear, crack, or rumple up a bit, but that just makes for more texture in the end. Layer on two more buttered sheets of phyllo across the bottom of the pan.

Butter the remaining phyllo as before, but begin placing the remaining sheets off-center around the pan so that their edges overlap in the center of the base and their other edges hang over the sides. Gently press the phyllo along the bottom and up the sides of the pan to create a crust. Transfer the filling to the phyllo crust and dot with the goat cheese or feta. Haphazardly gather and fold the overhanging phyllo over the edges of the filling, leaving the center exposed. Use any remaining butter to lightly brush this top crust.

Bake for 40 to 50 minutes, or until golden brown, crisp, and set in the center. Allow to cool slightly before removing from the pan and serving.

Note: If you're preparing the quiche ahead of time, cool it in the pan, cover, and store in the fridge for up to 3 days. Reheat in a 350°F oven for 15 to 20 minutes, or until the pastry is crisp and the center is warm.

A Toast to Soup

Super simple and ultra comforting, toast and soup are always there to help when things are feeling a little off.

Citrusy Goat Cheese Toast with Cherry Compote 38

Welsh Rarebit, a.k.a. Cheesy Toast 39

Seared Mushroom Ricotta Toast 42

Toast! All! Day!

It's a well-known fact that the university dining experience leaves a lot to be desired. Living on your own for the first time, you not only have to keep yourself on schedule and do your own laundry, you also have to learn the hard lesson that if you don't go to the grocery store, you'll be living off saltines and your roommate's jar of peanut butter, hoping she doesn't notice (Sorry, Megan!). It was during this time in my life that I really started to appreciate the glory of toast. Simple, quick, and satisfying from breakfast through dinner, toast is the perfect vehicle for any and every flavor you're craving.

I'd never pass up a good old-fashioned piece of toast first thing in the morning, but why settle for plain when you can smother it in cheesy, jammy goodness? Balancing the sharp tang of goat cheese spiked with citrus and cinnamon and the sweet juiciness of a quick cherry compote, this is the perfect wake-up call for your taste buds any day of the week.

Citrusy Goat Cheese Toast with Cherry Compote

SERVES 4

FOR THE COMPOTE

- 2 cups pitted fresh or frozen cherries, thawed if frozen
- ¼ cup sugar
- ¼ teaspoon cinnamon
- ½ medium orange, zested and juiced, divided
- ½ teaspoon cornstarch
- ¼ teaspoon almond or vanilla extract

FOR THE TOAST

- 5 oz chèvre or soft goat cheese
- 2 tablespoons cream, 10% or higher
- ½ orange, zested
- Pinch cinnamon
- 4 thick slices seedy or whole grain bread
- 2 tablespoons toasted sliced almonds, optional

For the compote, if using frozen cherries, drain away the liquid and reserve for a future use (hello, fun cocktail mix-in!). Place the cherries in a medium saucepan along with the sugar, cinnamon, and zest of the orange half. Place over medium heat and bring to a simmer. Turn the heat down to medium-low and cook for 10 to 15 minutes, just until the cherries are tender and juicy.

Meanwhile, add 1 tablespoon of orange juice in a small bowl and whisk in the cornstarch. Add this slurry to the cherry mixture and turn the heat up to medium. Bring to a simmer and cook for about 1 minute to thicken. Stir in the extract and set aside to cool slightly or fully to room temperature. This compote can be made up to 1 week in advance and stored in the fridge.

For the toast, place the chèvre or soft goat cheese in a bowl or small food processor. Add the cream and, using a whisk or the processor, beat or blitz to a smooth, spreadable consistency. Add the orange zest and cinnamon and mix just to combine.

Toast the bread to your liking, then spread the cheese mixture overtop. Top with the warm, room-temp, or chilled compote and scatter with the toasted almonds, if using.

Note: If you're not in the mood to make the cherry compote, swap it out for your favorite store-bought jam in any flavor you like, but don't skip on the orange zest and cinnamon. Simply stir them into the jam for a homemade feel.

Somewhere between an open-faced grilled cheese and creamy baked beer cheese dip, Welsh rarebit is essentially the ultimate form of cheesy toast. It's a staple in the UK, and I think it's about time that it travels across the pond to land on your next lunch table.

Welsh Rarebit, a.k.a. Cheesy Toast

SERVES 4

- 4 thick slices sourdough bread
- 8½–9 oz old white cheddar, grated
- ⅓ cup light or medium-bodied beer, such as ale
- 1 tablespoon Dijon or English mustard
- 1 teaspoon Worcestershire sauce
- 2–3 tablespoons chopped fresh chives, plus more for serving
- Pinch smoked paprika, plus more for serving
- Kosher salt
- Freshly ground black pepper
- 1 tablespoon butter, optional
- 4 eggs, optional

Place your oven rack in the top third of your oven and turn the broiler to high. Line a sheet pan with parchment paper.

Lightly toast the bread either under the broiler or in the toaster, then set aside on the lined sheet pan.

In a medium bowl, toss the cheddar, beer, mustard, Worcestershire, and chives together, and season with smoked paprika, salt, and pepper. Divide the cheese mixture over the toast and spread into an even layer.

Broil the cheesy toast until the topping is melted, bubbling, and deeply golden brown, about 5 minutes, being careful to keep an eye on it so that it doesn't burn.

If topping the toasts with eggs, place a large skillet over medium-high heat and melt the butter. Crack in the eggs and fry until crisp around the edges and the whites are set but the yolks are still runny.

Serve each piece of toast topped with an egg, if using, a scattering of chives, and a pinch of smoked paprika.

Note: With the addition of the egg, this dish technically becomes a buck rarebit, a variation on the Welsh original.

Seared Mushroom Ricotta Toast

Welsh Rarebit, a.k.a. Cheesy Toast
Citrusy Goat Cheese Toast with Cherry Compote

Hot, garlicky toast topped with a swipe of creamy Parmigiano-spiked ricotta and a pile of sweet, salty, savory, umami-y mushrooms is the perfect way to eat toast for dinner but still feel a little bit *fawncy.*

Seared Mushroom Ricotta Toast

SERVES 4

- 2 tablespoons olive oil
- 2 tablespoons soy sauce
- 2 tablespoons rice wine or white wine vinegar
- 2 tablespoons maple syrup
- 1 tablespoon Dijon mustard
- 3 garlic cloves, divided
- Freshly ground black pepper
- 14 oz oyster mushrooms
- 1 cup ricotta
- ½ cup finely grated Parmigiano-Reggiano
- Kosher salt
- 4 thick slices sourdough bread
- 2–3 tablespoons finely chopped fresh chives or parsley

In a large bowl, whisk together the olive oil, soy sauce, vinegar, maple syrup, and Dijon. Finely grate in two garlic cloves and season with pepper. Add the mushrooms, toss gently to coat, and set aside to marinate for 30 minutes or up to 2 hours.

Heat a large cast-iron skillet over medium-high. Working in batches if needed, remove the mushrooms from the marinade and add to the pan in a single layer, pressing down firmly with a spatula to give them a hard sear. Cook the mushrooms for 2 to 3 minutes per side, or until softened and caramelized around the edges.

Meanwhile, in a small bowl, stir the ricotta and Parmigiano-Reggiano together and season to taste with salt and pepper.

Toast the bread to your liking. Cut the end off the remaining garlic clove and rub the cut side onto the hot toast. Divide the ricotta mixture onto the toast and spread into an even layer. Spoon the mushrooms overtop and serve scattered with chives or parsley.

Note: Despite their appearance, mushrooms contain a lot of water. To get the best caramelization, don't overcrowd them in the pan.

It was during this time in my life that I really started to appreciate the glory of toast.

All-Clad

Nothing makes me feel more ready for the week and like I actually have my life together than this recipe. It's literally as easy as dumping things into a pot and letting them do their thing. It's a true Sunday soother, and you'll be rewarded with the best-smelling kitchen on the block and a pot full of ingredients just waiting to be turned into more kitchen magic.

Poached Chicken & Broth

MAKES 1 CHICKEN AND ABOUT 12 CUPS OF BROTH

- One 3 lb whole chicken
- 2 yellow onions, peeled and cut into large chunks
- 3 celery stalks, cut into large chunks
- 2 carrots, cut into large chunks
- 1 fennel bulb, optional
- 6 garlic cloves, peeled and smashed
- 1 handful fresh parsley stalks
- 2 teaspoons peppercorns
- 1½ teaspoons kosher salt
- 12 cups cold tap water

Place the chicken, onions, celery, carrots, fennel, garlic, parsley stalks, peppercorns, and salt into a large stockpot. Top with the cold tap water. Bring to a boil over high heat, then cover, turn the heat down to medium-low, and simmer for 1 to 1½ hours, or until the chicken is cooked through and the meat easily pulls away from the bone. While simmering, occasionally skim and discard any foam that rises to the surface.

Using a pair of tongs, carefully remove the chicken from the pot and transfer to a deep plate or large bowl. Don't worry if the chicken starts to fall apart—that just means you've got one heck of a delicious broth waiting for you in that pot! Set the chicken aside until cool enough to handle, about 20 minutes.

Meanwhile, strain the broth through a fine-mesh sieve and transfer to sealable containers. Allow the broth to cool to room temperature before storing in the fridge for up to 5 days or in the freezer for up to 3 months.

When the chicken is cool enough to handle, remove the skin and pull the meat from the bones. Transfer the meat to sealable containers and cool to room temperature before storing in the fridge for up to 4 days.

Note: Rather than using fresh veg in this recipe, save your vegetable scraps in a zip-top bag in the freezer and use them instead.

According to my driver's license, I'm an adult human and therefore need to consume things that contain vitamins. When that thought dawns on me, I tend to reach for something green. This soup, full of spinach and scattered with feta, is the perfect mix of healthy vitamins and my favorite food group: cheese.

Spanakopita Soup

SERVES 4

FOR THE CRISPY FETA TOPPER

4 sheets frozen phyllo, thawed
1–2 tablespoons butter, melted
2½–3½ oz crumbled feta
4 teaspoons sesame seeds

FOR THE SOUP

1 tablespoon butter
8 green onions, thinly sliced
2 garlic cloves, thinly sliced
Kosher salt
Freshly ground black pepper
1 lb cooking spinach or baby spinach (see note)
¼–½ teaspoon crushed red pepper flakes
Pinch freshly grated nutmeg
3½ cups chicken or vegetable broth (page 45 or store-bought)
1 lemon, zested
3–4 tablespoons chopped fresh dill
2 tablespoons chopped fresh parsley
½ cup cream

For the crispy feta topper, preheat your oven to 425°F and line a sheet pan with parchment paper. Lay out each sheet of phyllo on a work surface and brush with the melted butter. Scatter the crumbled feta and sesame seeds overtop, then lightly gather and bunch each sheet of phyllo into a rumpled pile. Transfer the phyllo piles to the sheet pan, leaving an inch or so between each, and bake for 15 minutes, or until golden and crisp.

Meanwhile, for the soup, place a large saucepan over medium-high heat. Add the butter, green onions, and garlic, season with salt and pepper, and cook for 1 to 2 minutes, or until the onions are lightly softened. Add the spinach and season with red pepper flakes, nutmeg, and a bit more salt and pepper. Add the broth and bring to a boil. Cook, stirring occasionally, until the spinach is tender and bright green, 3 to 4 minutes if using cooking spinach or 1 to 2 minutes if using baby spinach.

Stir in the lemon zest, dill, and parsley. Working in batches if necessary, transfer the soup to your blender, remove the vent cap, cover the lid with a kitchen towel to avoid splatter, and blitz until smooth. Return the soup to the pot, stir in the cream, season to taste with salt and pepper.

To serve, divide the soup into bowls and top with the crispy feta toppers.

Note: Cooking spinach is often sold in large bags near the bagged salad mixes at grocery stores. It is the grown-up version of baby spinach, which means it's a bit heartier and will last longer in your fridge. It's worth looking out for, as it's a fraction of the price of baby spinach, but if you cannot find it in a bag, you may be able to find bunches of spinach in the greens section of your produce aisle.

The glory of this soup is its bright green color—it's at its most verdant as soon as it's ready. While it will still be delicious, reheating the soup or keeping it on the heat for an extended period will mute this beautiful shade.

Pasta e fagioli is the veg-forward answer to a steaming pot of chicken noodle soup, mainly comprising, as the name says, pasta and beans. Like with many Italian dishes, the variations for this soup are endless, so the only thing I'm positive of is that my version will be nothing like the way Nonna used to make it.

Pasta e Fagioli

SERVES 4

- 6 cups chicken or vegetable broth (page 45 or store-bought)
- 2 tablespoons olive oil
- 1 yellow onion, diced
- 1 fennel bulb, diced, fronds reserved
- Kosher salt
- Freshly ground black pepper
- 2 garlic cloves, minced
- 1 can (19 fl oz) chickpeas or white kidney beans, drained and rinsed
- ¾ cup small dried pasta, such as acini di pepe, ditalini, or orzo
- 1 small wedge Parmigiano-Reggiano
- 2 large handfuls dark, leafy greens, such as Tuscan kale
- 2 tablespoons finely chopped fresh parsley
- 1 lemon, juiced
- Crushed red pepper flakes

In a medium saucepan, bring the broth to a simmer over medium heat.

Meanwhile, place a large saucepan over medium heat. Add the oil, onions, and fennel and season with salt and pepper. Cook, stirring occasionally, until the veg are tender and lightly golden around the edges, 5 to 7 minutes. Add the garlic and cook for 30 seconds, then add the chickpeas and dried pasta. Toast for 1 to 2 minutes, then carefully pour in the hot broth.

Cut the rind off the wedge of Parmigiano-Reggiano and add the rind to the pot. Turn the heat up to medium-high and bring to a boil. Cook just until the pasta is al dente.

Roughly chop the dark, leafy greens and add to the pot along with the parsley, lemon juice, and a few red pepper flakes to taste. Season with more salt and pepper as needed, and serve the soup topped with grated Parmigiano-Reggiano and fennel fronds.

Note: If leftovers are stored in the fridge, the pasta will continue to swell and absorb a good amount of the broth. This will give a sort of risotto-ish texture to the leftovers, which I love, but if you'd like to re-soup-ify the dish, just add a bit of broth when reheating.

This is probably very inside baseball, but there's a major divide in my house when it comes to the proper way to eat soup. While Aaron and Myra take their soup in a bowl, I'm firmly a mug gal paired with a big spoon, especially when it comes to a pot of pureed deliciousness.

Chive & Mushroom Soup

SERVES 4

- 2 tablespoons butter
- 1 yellow onion, diced
- Kosher salt
- Freshly ground black pepper
- 1 lb cremini mushrooms, sliced
- 3 garlic cloves, minced
- 1 tablespoon soy sauce
- ¼ cup dry white wine
- 3 cups chicken or vegetable broth (page 45 or store-bought)
- Freshly grated nutmeg
- ½ cup sour cream, plus more for serving
- ¼ cup thinly sliced fresh chives

In a large saucepan over medium heat, melt the butter. Add the onions, season with salt and pepper, and cook until softened and translucent, 5 to 7 minutes. Add the mushrooms, season with more salt and pepper, and continue to cook for another 5 to 7 minutes, or until the mushrooms and onions are golden brown. Stir in the garlic and cook for 30 seconds.

Deglaze the pan with the soy sauce and white wine, scraping the bottom of the pan to remove any stuck-on bits. Add the broth, season with a pinch of nutmeg, and bring to a simmer. Cover the pot and simmer for 10 to 15 minutes to bring the flavors together.

Working in batches if necessary, transfer the soup to your blender, remove the vent cap, cover the lid with a kitchen towel to avoid splatter, and blitz the soup until smooth. Return the soup to the pot, stir in the sour cream, and turn the heat down to low to keep the soup warm.

Serve the soup topped with a dollop of sour cream, lots of chives, and a pinch of black pepper and nutmeg.

Does anyone else get cravings so strong that the only way to get your brain to think about literally anything else is to give into it? That sometimes happens to me when a hunger for Indian food strikes. Our favorite Indian takeout spot is way too close to justify delivery, so on those days when we're hankering for some of that signature warmth but *really* don't want to leave the house even for a 5-minute walk, you'll find this stew with curry inspired flavors bubbling away on the stove.

Curry Spiced Sweet Potato & Chickpea Stew

SERVES 4

FOR THE STEW

2 large sweet potatoes
1 red onion
Olive oil
Kosher salt
Freshly ground black pepper
1 can (19 fl oz) chickpeas
3 garlic cloves, minced
3–4 tablespoons finely grated fresh ginger
2–3 teaspoons curry powder
1½ teaspoons ground turmeric
1 teaspoon ground cumin
½ teaspoon ground coriander
¼–½ teaspoon cayenne pepper
1 can (5 fl oz) tomato paste
4 cups vegetable broth
1 can (14 fl oz) coconut milk
3 cups chopped dark, leafy greens
1 lemon, juiced

FOR THE FLATBREADS

1½–2 cups all-purpose flour
1 teaspoon baking powder
½ teaspoon kosher salt
¾ cup plain yogurt
¼ cup warm water

FOR SERVING

Plain yogurt
Cherry tomatoes, quartered
Fresh cilantro leaves

Preheat your oven to 400°F.

For the stew, peel and dice the sweet potatoes and cut the onion into wedges. Add to a sheet pan, toss with 2 tablespoons of olive oil, and season with salt and pepper. Roast for 25 minutes, or until the sweet potatoes and onions are caramelized and softened.

Meanwhile, place a large saucepan over medium heat. Drain and rinse the chickpeas, and add to the pan along with 2 teaspoons of olive oil, and the garlic, ginger, curry powder, turmeric, cumin, coriander, and cayenne pepper. Season with salt and pepper and cook, stirring often, for 1 to 2 minutes to toast the spices and bring the flavors together. Stir in the tomato paste and cook for 1 minute, then add a splash of the broth to deglaze the pan, scraping the bottom to lift off any stuck-on bits. Stir in the remaining broth and the coconut milk and bring to a simmer. Add the greens and cook for about 5 minutes, or until tender.

Remove the sweet potatoes and onions from the oven and smash about half into a smooth-ish mash. Add all the roasted veg to the pot and stir through. Simmer for at least 2 minutes to bring the flavors together and thicken the stew. Finish with the lemon juice and a final seasoning of salt and pepper, if needed.

For the flatbreads, in a large bowl, combine 1½ cups of flour with the baking powder and salt. Add the yogurt and warm water and mix into a shaggy dough. Knead the dough for about 1 minute, adding more flour as needed, until a smooth dough forms. Set aside to rest for 10 minutes.

Heat a large cast-iron skillet over medium heat. Divide the dough into four or six pieces and roll out each to about ¼ inch thick on a floured work surface. Cook the flatbreads one at a time in the dry skillet, flipping once, until cooked through and golden spots appear.

Serve the stew topped with some yogurt, cherry tomatoes, and cilantro, with a piece of flatbread on the side.

By smashing half of the roasted sweet potatoes, you're releasing more of their starches, which will help thicken the stew. If you want it even thicker, you can also squash some of the chickpeas against the side of the pot.

Poached dumplings like this never seem like they should work. With a loose dough that's almost drop biscuit-y, you'd think they'd fall apart into soggy nothingness as they cook, but this, my friend, is kitchen wizardry at its finest.

Chicken, Sausage & Dumplings

SERVES 8

- 2 tablespoons butter
- 2 (3½ oz each) Italian sausages, spicy or mild
- 1 yellow onion, diced
- 2 carrots, diced
- 1 celery stalk, diced
- ½ fennel bulb, diced
- Kosher salt
- Freshly ground black pepper
- 8 cups chicken broth (page 45 or store-bought)
- 1 cooked whole chicken (page 45 or store-bought rotisserie)
- 1½ cups all-purpose flour
- 2 teaspoons baking powder
- ¾ cup buttermilk
- 3 tablespoons finely chopped fresh parsley, divided
- ½ cup cream, optional
- 1 teaspoon Dijon mustard

In a large pot over medium heat, melt the butter. Transfer 1 tablespoon of the melted butter to a small bowl and set aside.

Using a sharp knife, split open the sausage casings and remove the meat. Discard the casings and add the sausage meat to the pot. Using a wooden spoon, break up the sausage meat and cook until lightly golden and cooked through, 6 to 8 minutes. Use a slotted spoon to remove the sausage meat from the pot and set aside.

Add the diced onions, carrots, celery, and fennel to the pot, season with salt and pepper, and cook for 4 to 5 minutes, or until softened and lightly golden brown. Carefully pour in the broth and bring to a boil for 10 minutes.

Meanwhile, remove the skin from the chicken and pull the meat from the bones. Using two forks, shred the meat into large bite-sized hunks and set aside.

To make the dumpling dough, in a large bowl, stir together the flour, baking powder, and ¾ teaspoon of salt. Add the buttermilk, the reserved melted butter, and 2 tablespoons of parsley. Stir just to combine.

Add the chicken and sausage meat to the pot and stir in the cream, if using, Dijon, and remaining 1 tablespoon of parsley. Season to taste with salt and pepper.

Using two spoons or a small spring-loaded ice cream scoop, drop small dumplings into the pot, leaving some space between each. The dumplings will grow quite a bit as they cook, so I usually aim for each dumpling to be about 1 heaped tablespoon of dough. Cover the pot with a lid, turn the heat down to low, and cook for 15 minutes, or until the dumplings are cooked through.

Serve the soup immediately.

Does anyone else have the same issue as I have, where they are incapable of making the correct amount of rice? Without fail, I will make about eighteen times too much, resulting in tubs and tubs of leftovers. To deal with the Tupperware tower in my fridge, I've come up with recipes that use precooked rice as an ingredient. Cabbage rolls chip away at the stack and are one of Aaron's favorite dishes, but they tend to be a bit of a project to put together. With this soup, you polish off some of that rice and get all the flavors of cabbage rolls without the fuss.

Kinda Cabbage Roll, Kinda Tomato Soup

SERVES 6

2 tablespoons butter
3½ oz kielbasa, diced
1 yellow onion, diced
1 carrot, diced
2 celery stalks, diced
1 lb lean ground beef
Kosher salt
Freshly ground black pepper
3 garlic cloves, minced
2 teaspoons dried thyme
1 teaspoon ground cumin
4 cups beef or vegetable broth
1 can (26 fl oz) crushed tomatoes
3 cups chopped savoy cabbage
1 cup cooked rice
2 tablespoons chopped fresh parsley
2 tablespoons chopped fresh dill, plus more for serving
Sour cream, for serving

In a large pot over medium heat, melt the butter. Add the kielbasa and cook, stirring often, until golden brown and a little crispy, about 3 minutes. Using a slotted spoon, remove the kielbasa and set aside.

Add the onions, carrots, celery, and beef to the pot, season with salt and pepper, and cook for 6 to 8 minutes, or until the vegetables are lightly softened and the beef is golden brown and cooked through. Stir in the garlic, thyme, and cumin and cook for 30 seconds. Add the broth and crushed tomatoes, turn the heat up to medium-high, and bring to a boil. Add the cabbage and rice and boil for to 10 minutes, or until tender. Turn the heat down to low, stir in the parsley and dill, and season with more salt and pepper, if needed.

Serve topped with a dollop of sour cream, the crispy kielbasa, and a bit of fresh dill.

GOOD
DAYS
TRAIL

Snack Town

Your one-stop destination for world-famous dippy, crispy, and cheesy things!

During my time at university, I learned the usual stuff, like a weird amount of knowledge about postmodern literature and Russian history, but the day-to-day lessons like "If you don't do your laundry, you won't have any clean socks" tend to come up more frequently in my actual life. One lesson I'll never forget came from my friend Laura Baldwick. She is the culinary genius who schooled me in Light Night Snacking 101. While I've always been a chip gal and am a perennial pickle lover, I'd never had a dill pickle chip before meeting Laura! Her go-to was a bag of Old Dutch Rip-L Creamy Dill potato chips, and once I had my first crunch, I never looked back. With this dip—a cross between tzatziki, ranch, and a bowl of pickles—I think I've graduated to PhD-level snacking.

Pickle Dip

MAKES ABOUT 2 CUPS

FOR THE DIP

½ cup grated dill pickles
1 cup plain Greek yogurt
¼ cup mayonnaise
½ lemon, zested and juiced
½ teaspoon onion powder
½ teaspoon garlic powder
2 tablespoons chopped fresh dill
2 tablespoons chopped fresh chives
Kosher salt
Freshly ground black pepper

FOR SERVING

4 Greek pitas
Canola oil
Kosher salt

Place the grated pickles in a sieve lined with paper towel and set over the sink to drain.

Meanwhile, in a medium bowl, whisk together the yogurt, mayonnaise, lemon zest, lemon juice, onion powder, garlic powder, dill, and chives.

Gather the paper towel up around the pickles and firmly squeeze to remove as much moisture as possible. Add the pickles to the yogurt mixture and stir well to combine. Season to taste with salt and lots of pepper and set aside in the fridge.

For serving, cut each pita into eight wedges. Pour about ½ inch of oil into a large heavy-bottomed pot and place over medium heat. When the oil is hot and bubbles form around a wooden spoon when submerged in the oil, add the pitas in batches and fry until golden on both sides, flipping once. Transfer the fried pitas to a sheet pan lined with a rack and continue frying until all are crisp and golden brown. Scatter the hot pitas with salt. Allow the pitas to cool slightly, then serve with the dip. If you like, you can garnish the dip with dill, pepper, and a pickle.

Note: For the real pickle enthusiasts, skip the fried pitas and serve this dip with some crinkle-cut dill pickle potato chips.

DAYS

There is something so magical about this absurdly named berry. First off, yes, an eggplant is botanically a berry, which is wild, but also, whoever saw it and thought "eggs"? I guess two wild things balance each other out? By broiling and then slowly roasting the eggplant, you end up with a smoky, almost custardy canvas that's perfect for painting with punchy flavors.

Smoky Harissa Eggplant Dip

MAKES ABOUT 2 CUPS

- 1 large Italian eggplant
- Olive oil
- Kosher salt
- Freshly ground black pepper
- 1 garlic head
- 1 lemon, zested and juiced
- ¼ cup tahini
- ¼ cup chopped walnuts
- ½ cup crumbled feta, plus more for serving
- 2 tablespoons chopped fresh parsley, plus more for serving
- 2–4 teaspoons harissa paste
- ½ teaspoon smoked paprika, plus more for serving
- ½ teaspoon ground cumin, plus more for serving

Place your oven rack in the middle position and turn the broiler to high. Cut the eggplant in half lengthwise and transfer to a sheet pan, cut side up. Drizzle with a little olive oil and season with salt and pepper. Broil for 12 to 15 minutes, or until lightly charred.

Meanwhile, cut the top off the head of garlic and place the garlic on a square of aluminum foil, cut side up. Drizzle with olive oil, season with salt and pepper, and wrap the garlic up.

Once the eggplant has broiled, flip it over so that it is cut side down and add the garlic bundle to the sheet pan. Set the oven temperature to 375°F and roast for 35 to 40 minutes, or until the eggplant is wrinkled and deflated and the garlic is softened. Set the eggplant and garlic aside to cool slightly.

Once cooled, scoop the eggplant flesh from the skin and transfer to your food processor or high-speed blender. Add as much of the roasted garlic as you'd like, along with the lemon zest, lemon juice, tahini, walnuts, feta, parsley, harissa, smoked paprika, and cumin. Season with salt and pepper and process until it's as smooth as you'd like. If desired, drizzle in a few tablespoons of olive oil for extra creaminess.

Transfer the dip to a serving bowl and top with a glug of oil, a little more paprika and cumin, and a scattering of feta and parsley, if desired. For a bit more heat, drizzle a bit of extra harissa overtop as well.

Note: Homemade flatbreads are the perfect pairing with this dip (recipe on page 52 with the Curry Spiced Sweet Potato & Chickpea Stew).

Anytime someone asks what my favorite food is, my honest answer is and always will be soda crackers. I know that may come as a shock and make you rethink your trust in my cooking abilities, but no matter what mood I'm in, a soda cracker is always there.

Butter Baked Saltines

SERVES 6 TO 8

- 1 sleeve (about 36) soda crackers, salted or unsalted
- ¼ cup butter, melted
- Kosher salt, optional
- Freshly ground black pepper, optional

Preheat your oven to 400°F.

Lay the crackers on a sheet pan in a single layer and brush with the melted butter. If you have any butter left over, evenly drizzle it over the crackers. Season with salt (if not using salted crackers) and a bit of pepper, if desired.

Bake for 5 to 8 minutes, or until golden brown.

The crackers can be stored in a container or zip-top bag at room temperature for up to 3 days. If they get a little soft, just heat them in a 400°F oven for a few minutes until crisp.

Note: For added flavor, mix a little garlic powder and dried herbs into the melted butter and scatter the crackers with some finely grated Parmigiano-Reggiano before baking.

BEER · BIÈRE

Aaron and I had a grand old time at our wedding, but if we had the chance for a redo, we'd take a page from the playbook of our friends Kyle and Renée. Having eloped in Denmark, they threw a great party a few months later, containing all the hits and none of the misses of a traditional wedding day. There was no stress to pick a bridal party, no officiant writing the wrong name on the contract (something that happened to a friend of mine!), and no forced smoochin' in front of all your friends and family. It was just their best people hanging out at a brewery for the night, digging into deep-fried cheese curds, the secret ingredient to any marriage.

Fried Cheese Curds with Chipotle Ranch

SERVES 4 TO 6

FOR THE CHIPOTLE RANCH

½ cup sour cream

¼ cup mayonnaise

2 chipotle peppers in adobo sauce

1 lemon, juiced

1 teaspoon onion powder

½ teaspoon garlic powder

2 tablespoons chopped fresh dill

Kosher salt

Freshly ground black pepper

FOR THE CHEESE CURDS

Canola oil

7–9 oz cheddar cheese curds (see note)

¾ cup all-purpose flour

½ cup cornstarch

1 teaspoon baking powder

1 teaspoon kosher salt

¼ teaspoon freshly ground black pepper

¼ teaspoon garlic powder

⅔ cup lager or light-flavored ale

For the chipotle ranch, in a small food processor or smoothie blender, combine the sour cream, mayonnaise, chipotle peppers in adobo sauce, lemon juice, onion powder, and garlic powder and blitz until smooth. Transfer the dip to a serving dish, stir in the dill, and season with salt and pepper. Set aside.

For the cheese curds, pour about 3 inches of oil into a large heavy-bottomed pot and place over medium heat. Line a sheet pan with paper towel or a cooling rack and set aside.

Meanwhile, dump the cheese curds into a large bowl and separate any large chunks. Add the flour and toss to evenly coat. Transfer the curds to a fine-mesh sieve and shake over the large bowl to remove any excess flour, catching the flour back in the bowl. Set the curds aside.

Add the cornstarch to the flour along with the baking powder, salt, pepper, and garlic powder and whisk to combine. Pour in the beer and whisk into a smooth batter. Scatter about half of the cheese curds into the batter and toss lightly to coat.

When the oil is hot and bubbles form when a wooden spoon is gently submerged in the oil, use two forks to lift the cheese curds out of the batter and transfer to the hot oil. Fry for 1 to 2 minutes, just until crisp and very lightly golden, then transfer to the prepared sheet pan. Repeat to coat the remaining cheese curds in the batter and fry them in the hot oil. Serve immediately with the chipotle ranch.

Note: Cheese curds are, unfortunately for the rest of the world, hard to find outside Canada. If you can't find them, substitute with chunks or ½-inch-thick sticks of brick mozzarella.

Whenever we have people coming over, whether for a low- or high-key hang, brie is always on the menu. I've served it straight from the fridge (against my better judgment), baked, and even fried. But in the summer, this is my go-to. Smoky, oozy, and totally delicious, grilled brie is the easiest way to wow.

Grilled Tomatoes & Brie

SERVES 6 TO 8

1 pint cherry tomatoes
2 garlic cloves, minced
Olive oil
Kosher salt
Freshly ground black pepper
1 wheel (12–14 oz) brie (see note)
1 tablespoon red wine or balsamic vinegar
¼ cup chopped fresh basil
2 tablespoons chopped fresh parsley
Crostini or crusty bread, for serving

Place a piece of aluminum foil under the rack of your barbecue and heat it to medium-high.

In a large bowl, combine the cherry tomatoes and garlic. Toss with a tablespoon of olive oil and season with salt and pepper. Transfer the tomatoes to a vegetable grill pan or a piece of aluminum foil with the edges slightly turned up. Place on the barbecue, close the lid, and cook for 2 to 3 minutes while you prepare the brie.

Lightly drizzle the brie with a few teaspoons of olive oil. Place the wheel directly onto the barbecue rack, close the lid, and cook alongside the tomatoes for 3 to 5 minutes, or until grill marks appear but the brie is still a bit firm. Using a large metal spatula, carefully flip the wheel over.

At this point, if your tomatoes are looking a little charred and juicy, remove them from the grill. If not, leave them on the grill and continue to cook alongside the brie until the cheese is soft but you are still able to lift it. Transfer the brie to a serving platter and set aside.

Transfer the tomatoes back to the bowl and toss with the vinegar and a little more oil. Add the basil and parsley and season to taste with salt and pepper. Spoon the warm tomatoes over the brie and serve alongside some crostini or crusty bread.

Note: There are so many reasons why I love grilling brie, but topping the list is the fact that you actually want to use a cheaper wheel here. Those more economical wheels of brie are often firmer and less oozy, allowing them to hold up against the high heat of the grill, so put the fancy stuff back on the shelf and opt for the grocery store brand.

Finally, an answer to the unsolvable question of blue cheese or ranch. This is the best of both worlds for the dip enthusiast in your life.

Crispy Baked Buffalo Wings with Blue Cheese Ranch

SERVES 4 TO 6

FOR THE WINGS

2¼ lb chicken wings

1 tablespoon canola oil

1 tablespoon cornstarch

1 teaspoon kosher salt

¼ teaspoon freshly ground black pepper

¼ teaspoon garlic powder

FOR THE BUFFALO SAUCE

¼ cup butter, melted

½ cup cayenne pepper hot sauce, such as Frank's RedHot

1 tablespoon honey

FOR THE BLUE CHEESE RANCH

½ cup buttermilk

3 tablespoons sour cream

3 tablespoons mayonnaise

1 tablespoon finely chopped fresh dill

1 tablespoon finely chopped fresh parsley

1 tablespoon finely chopped fresh chives

1 teaspoon onion powder

⅓ cup crumbled blue cheese, preferably Danish blue

Kosher salt

Freshly ground black pepper

For the wings, preheat your oven to 425°F and line a sheet pan with a wire rack.

Using a few pieces of paper towel, dry the chicken wings very well. Place them in a large bowl and toss with the oil.

In a small bowl, stir together the cornstarch, salt, pepper, and garlic powder. Scatter the seasoning over the wings and toss well to coat.

Transfer the wings to the prepared sheet pan and roast for 25 minutes. Reduce the temperature to 250°F and continue to roast for 15 to 20 minutes, or until the wings are cooked through, golden brown, and crisp.

Meanwhile, prepare the buffalo sauce. In a small pot over low heat, whisk together the melted butter, hot sauce, and honey. Keep warm.

For the blue cheese ranch, in a small bowl, whisk together the buttermilk, sour cream, mayonnaise, dill, parsley, chives, and onion powder. Stir in the blue cheese and season with salt and lots of pepper.

Transfer the cooked wings to a large bowl, pour the warm buffalo sauce overtop, and toss well to combine and evenly coat. Serve immediately with the dip.

Note: The two-temperature cook in this recipe is key to crispy baked wings. The initial high heat of the oven renders the fat in the chicken wings, allowing them to get crispy without a fryer, while the lower finishing temperature cooks the wings while keeping them juicy.

Remember those commercials for a certain seafood restaurant that's arguably more famous for its biscuits than any of its seafood? One commercial in particular stands out in my memory. It was for all-you-can-eat shrimp with various preparations of those little crustaceans flying and bouncing across the screen in extreme close-up. Being a lifelong shrimp fanatic, I'm kind of drooling just thinking about it . . . good thing this recipe's here.

Grilled Shrimp Cocktail with Herby Aioli

SERVES 6 TO 8

FOR THE HERBY AIOLI

- 4 garlic cloves, minced
- ½ lemon, juiced
- ½ cup mayonnaise
- ½ teaspoon Dijon mustard
- ¼ cup chopped fresh fine herbs, such as chives, parsley, basil, and/or tarragon
- Kosher salt
- Freshly ground black pepper

FOR THE SHRIMP

- 2¼ lb raw peeled shrimp, 21–25 count (see note)
- ½ lemon, zested and juiced
- 3 tablespoons olive oil
- 4 garlic cloves, reserved from the aioli
- Kosher salt
- Freshly ground black pepper
- Lemon wedge, for serving

Preheat your grill or a grill pan to medium.

For the herby aioli, place the garlic in a small bowl and pour in the lemon juice. Set aside for 5 minutes to allow the garlic to infuse the lemon juice. In a separate bowl, combine the mayonnaise, Dijon, and herbs. Place a strainer over the bowl and pour in the garlic-infused lemon juice, setting the garlic aside to use in the shrimp marinade. Mix the aioli well to combine, then season to taste with salt and pepper.

For the shrimp, place the shrimp in a large bowl and add the lemon zest, lemon juice, and oil. Add the reserved garlic from the aioli and season with salt and pepper. Toss well to combine and set aside for 5 minutes.

Place the shrimp on the grill and cook for 2 to 3 minutes per side, or until pink and plump.

If serving the shrimp hot, simply transfer from the grill to a serving platter and serve with the aioli. If serving cold, chill in the fridge and serve over ice with the aioli and a lemon wedge on the side.

Note: Ever wonder what the number listed on a bag of shrimp means? Well, it indicates the size of the shrimp by estimating how many you'll get per pound. The bigger the number, the smaller the shrimp. The smaller the number, the bigger the shrimp.

SHRIMP COCKTAIL

Gooey and cheesy with a golden-brown crunch, arancini are the ultimate Italian use-em-up treat. They are delicious fresh from the oil, but you can easily make them ahead and reheat them in the oven, making them the perfect snack for your next at-home hang.

Arancini

MAKES 6

- ¼ cup all-purpose flour
- 1 egg, beaten
- ½ cup panko or traditional breadcrumbs
- ¼ teaspoon Italian seasoning
- Kosher salt
- 1½ cups prepared risotto (see note)
- 6 cubes (about ⅓ inch each) brick mozzarella
- Canola oil
- Flaky sea salt
- Prepared tomato sauce, optional

Set out a small sheet pan and fill a small bowl with water.

Set out three separate bowls or shallow dishes. Place the flour in one, the beaten egg in another, and the breadcrumbs and Italian seasoning in the third. Season the flour and breadcrumbs with salt and stir to combine.

Lightly dampen your hands and scoop ¼ cup of the prepared risotto into your hands. Flatten the risotto slightly and place a cube of mozzarella in the center. Wrap and pinch the risotto around the cheese to form a ball and fully enclose the cheese. Place the arancini ball onto the sheet pan and continue until you have used up all the risotto and cheese.

Working with one at a time, toss the arancini in the flour, then in the egg, and finally roll in the breadcrumb mixture. Place the breaded arancini back onto the sheet pan. Once they're all coated, place the arancini in the fridge or freezer for 10 minutes while you heat the oil.

In a small saucepan or high-sided skillet, heat about 1 inch of canola oil over medium heat until it reaches 350°F (when the oil is hot enough, a small sprinkling of breadcrumbs will brown in about 10 seconds). Retrieve the arancini from the fridge and, working in batches so as not to overcrowd the pan, carefully fry until deeply golden brown, about 4 to 5 minutes, flipping occasionally. Transfer the arancini to a rack-lined sheet pan and season immediately with flaky sea salt.

Serve as is or with prepared tomato sauce.

Note: Any leftover risotto works perfectly in these arancini, but if you're looking for a new recipe, give my Cacio e Pepe Risotto (page 131) or Get Your Greens Risotto (page 132) a try.

Starch City

Population: Bread & Potatoes

Bacon & Rosemary Biscuits with Bacon Honey Butter 81

Garlic Parmesan Biscuits 84

Chocolate Orange Biscuits 85

Biscuits 3 Ways

To me, comfort sometimes means being able to make something bready in a flash when the bin is bare. I mean, they are called "quick breads" for a reason.

Note: You can make each of the biscuit recipes by folding the dough for extra layers or by using two large spoons to drop mounds of dough straight onto the sheet pan for a fluffier interior. Baking time and temperature remain the same, so the choice is yours.

I don't think I'd be able to be friends with someone who doesn't like biscuits.

I have a few go-to recipes for when someone pops by for a cozy at home hang, but biscuits are my number one. They're quick and easy to throw together, and I actually don't think I'd be able to be friends with someone who doesn't like them. These babies are perfect for any time of day, and they're made even more craveable with the addition of bacon, rosemary, and an over-the-top buttery spread.

Bacon & Rosemary Biscuits with Bacon Honey Butter

MAKES 9

FOR THE BISCUITS

6 slices bacon

2 cups all-purpose flour

4 teaspoons baking powder

¼ teaspoon baking soda

1 teaspoon kosher salt

¼ teaspoon freshly ground black pepper

¼ cup cold butter

2 tablespoons finely chopped fresh rosemary

1–1¼ cups cold buttermilk

FOR THE BACON HONEY BUTTER

⅓ cup butter, room temperature

2–3 tablespoons honey

2 tablespoons bacon fat, reserved from biscuits

Flaky salt, to taste

For the biscuits, line two sheet pans with parchment paper.

Lay the bacon on one of the parchment-lined sheet pans and place in your cold oven. Set the oven to 425°F, and once the oven is heated, set a timer for 6 minutes. Check the bacon for crispness. If golden and crisp, remove from the oven and transfer the bacon to a piece of paper towel to cool. If the bacon is still a bit wobbly, continue to cook, checking every 2 minutes or so, until crisp. Keep the oven on and reserve 4 tablespoons of bacon fat.

In a large bowl, whisk together the flour, baking powder, baking soda, salt, and pepper. Cut the butter into pats and toss in the flour mixture. Using your fingers, snap and rub in the butter until the pieces are about the size of peas. Chop the bacon and add it to the mixture. Add the rosemary and toss to combine. Make a well in the center, pour in 1 cup of buttermilk, and stir to combine. The dough should hold together but still be a bit crumbly. If needed, add another splash of buttermilk.

Lightly flour a work surface and scoop handfuls of the dough out, stacking them into a rough tower. Scatter the top with flour and press down to about 1 inch thick. Fold the dough over onto itself and repeat this pressing and folding process two to three more times to build flaky layers. Press the dough into a 1-inch-thick rectangle and cut into nine equal biscuits. Transfer to the second parchment-lined sheet pan and brush the tops of the biscuits with 2 tablespoons of the reserved bacon fat. If time allows, chill the biscuits in the freezer for about 10 minutes.

Bake the biscuits for 15 to 18 minutes, or until risen and golden brown.

Meanwhile, make the bacon honey butter. In a small bowl, beat the butter with the honey and remaining 2 tablespoons of reserved bacon fat. Season to taste with flaky salt.

Allow the biscuits to cool slightly, then serve warm with lots of bacon honey butter.

Note: A cup of grated cheese like cheddar or Gruyère would be a delish addition to these biscuits. Just mix it into the dough along with the bacon and rosemary.

Garlic Parmesan Biscuits

Bacon & Rosemary Biscuits with Bacon Honey Butter
Chocolate Orange Biscuits

Almost every year since I was born, my family has loaded into our station wagon stuffed to the gills with luggage, beach gear, and ample car snacks to head down to Kiawah Island in South Carolina. We have countless stories of summers past, like when my Aunt Joanie put a horseshoe crab on her head, or when my dad chased my, unbeknownst to him, empty stroller down the beach, thinking that the wind was stealing his brand-new baby. The excitement of these trips starts well before we set foot on that beautiful island. On the drive down, we always stop for the night in Morgantown, West Virginia. It's the perfect midpoint for a rest, and it used to have this little hole-in-the-wall restaurant with *the best. buns. ever.* Sadly, Puglioni's has closed its doors, but the memory of those buns lives rent-free in my mind. Doused in herby garlic butter and ground Parm, these biscuits are a quick and easy way to get those family road-trip vibes at home without having to dig out my passport.

Garlic Parmesan Biscuits

MAKES 9

FOR THE BISCUITS

2 cups all-purpose flour

4 teaspoons baking powder

¼ teaspoon baking soda

1 teaspoon kosher salt

½ teaspoon garlic powder

¼ cup cold butter

¾ cup finely grated Parmigiano-Reggiano (see note)

1–1¼ cups cold buttermilk

FOR THE GARLIC BUTTER

¼ cup butter, melted

1 garlic clove, minced

1 tablespoon finely chopped fresh parsley

¼ cup ground Parmigiano-Reggiano (see note)

For the biscuits, preheat your oven to 425°F and line a sheet pan with parchment paper.

In a large bowl, whisk the flour, baking powder, baking soda, salt, and garlic powder together. Cut the butter into pats and toss in the flour mixture. Using your fingers, snap and rub in the butter until the pieces are about the size of peas. Stir in the Parmigiano-Reggiano. Make a well in the center, pour in 1 cup of the buttermilk, and stir to combine. The dough should hold together but still be a bit crumbly. If needed, add another splash of buttermilk.

Lightly flour a work surface and scoop handfuls of the dough out, stacking them into a rough tower. Scatter the top with flour and press down to about 1 inch thick. Fold the dough over onto itself and repeat this pressing and folding process two to three more times to build flaky layers. Press the dough into a 1-inch-thick rectangle, cut into nine equal biscuits, and transfer to the sheet pan. If time allows, chill the biscuits in the freezer for 10 minutes.

Bake the biscuits for 14 to 16 minutes, or until risen and golden brown.

Meanwhile, make the garlic butter. In a small bowl, stir together the melted butter, garlic, and parsley.

When the biscuits are done, brush the garlic butter overtop and scatter with the Parmigiano-Reggiano. Return the biscuits to the oven for 2 minutes to allow the garlic butter to melt into the biscuits and the cheese to stick to the tops. Serve immediately.

In the world of individually sized quick breads, there are two main camps: scones and biscuits. Typically, biscuits are reserved for more savory applications while scones take on a sweet role, but I'm not going to lie: I've always preferred pretty much everything about biscuits. Scones use less butter and the dough is often worked more thoroughly. As a result, they have a shorter (more crumbly) texture, whereas biscuits are lighter, fluffier, and, obviously, more buttery. By adding sweet flavors into a standard biscuit dough along with just a touch of sugar, you get the best of both worlds. A sweet treat with, in my personal opinion, optimal texture.

Chocolate Orange Biscuits

MAKES 9

- 2 cups all-purpose flour
- 4 teaspoons baking powder
- ¼ teaspoon baking soda
- 1 teaspoon kosher salt
- 1 tablespoon sugar
- ½ cup cold butter
- ½ cup chopped dark chocolate
- 1–1¼ cups cold buttermilk
- 1 orange, zested
- 1 tablespoon turbinado sugar, optional

Preheat your oven to 425°F and line a sheet pan with parchment paper.

In a large bowl, whisk the flour, baking powder, baking soda, salt, and sugar together. Cut the butter into pats and toss in the flour mixture. Using your fingers, snap and rub in the butter until the pieces are about the size of peas. Toss in the chocolate.

Measure out 1 cup of buttermilk and stir in the orange zest to combine. Make a well in the center of the dry ingredients, pour in the buttermilk, and stir to combine. The dough should hold together but still be a bit shaggy. If needed, add another splash of buttermilk.

Using two spoons or a spring-loaded scoop, scoop and drop nine equal portions of the biscuit dough onto the prepared sheet pan. Scatter with the turbinado sugar, if using. If time allows, chill the biscuits in the freezer for 10 minutes.

Bake the biscuits for 15 to 18 minutes, or until risen and golden brown. Serve warm or at room temperature.

Note: If the classic combo of chocolate and orange isn't your favorite, swap out the orange zest for lemon and the dark chocolate for white, and toss in a cup of fresh blueberries.

Jelly Doughnut Focaccia 95
Baked Brie Focaccia 88
Pretzel Focaccia with Beer Cheese 89

Focaccia 4 Ways

For those among us who like the *idea* of baking homemade bread but can't be bothered with starters, lames, and oven springs, focaccia is the loaf for you.

Note: The dough in the focaccia recipes might seem a bit sticky after the first mix, but don't be tempted to keep adding flour. As you stretch and fold the dough over onto itself in the bowl (a.k.a. a bowl fold), the dough will start to come together as the gluten develops. Just don't forget to dampen your hands before you start a bowl fold—it makes things a lot less messy!

Is anyone else's algorithm essentially just Nora Ephron–style kitchens, bird content, and bread baking? Just me? While making my own sourdough starter and baking perfect, crusty loaves eludes me, I've found that focaccia is the bread that fits my lifestyle. I've been making pans of the stuff for years but have finally figured out the perfect low-knead, light and bubbly focaccia of my dreams. And what could be wrong with adding the perennial flavors of a classic baked brie into the mix?

Baked Brie Focaccia

MAKES ONE 9-INCH SQUARE LOAF

3¼ cups bread flour
2¼ teaspoons (1 packet) instant yeast
1½ teaspoons kosher salt
1 teaspoon sugar
2 sprigs fresh rosemary, divided
1½ cups warm water
7 tablespoons olive oil, divided
4 garlic cloves, divided
About 5 oz brie, diced
Flaky sea salt
Freshly ground black pepper

Note: For a plain focaccia loaf, omit the garlic and rosemary in the dough and simply top the loaf with olive oil and flaky salt before baking.

In a large bowl, combine the bread flour, yeast, salt, and sugar. Strip the leaves from one sprig of rosemary and finely chop them up. Add the chopped rosemary to the dry ingredients, stir to combine, and make a well in the center. Add the warm water and 3 tablespoons of olive oil. Grate in two garlic cloves. Using a wooden spoon, stir for 1 to 2 minutes, until a stretchy, wet dough forms.

Grease a large clean bowl with 1 tablespoon of olive oil and transfer the dough to the bowl. Cover with a piece of plastic wrap or a dinner plate and set aside in a warm spot for 15 minutes.

After 15 minutes, dampen your hands and lift and stretch the dough onto itself a few times, working your way around the dough about two times and bringing the edges into the center. The dough should firm up a bit and be less sticky once you've done this turn. Flip the dough over so that it is seam side down, re-cover the bowl, and set aside in the warm spot for 30 minutes. Repeat the folding process one more time, then cover and set aside for 1 hour, or until the dough is doubled in size.

Add 1 tablespoon of oil to a 9-inch square baking pan. Transfer the dough to the pan and lightly stretch it into the corners, being careful not to punch all the air out. Gently cover the pan with a clean kitchen towel and set aside in the warm spot for 45 minutes to 1 hour, until puffy.

Preheat your oven to 425°F. Dampen your fingers with water or a little oil and press them into the dough to dimple the surface, pressing all the way through to the pan. Thinly slice the remaining two cloves of garlic and pick the leaves from the remaining rosemary sprig. Place the garlic and rosemary in a bowl, toss with the remaining 2 tablespoons of oil, and drizzle over the focaccia. Scatter the brie over the dimples in the focaccia. Season with flaky salt and a pinch of pepper.

Bake for 20 to 22 minutes, or until golden and springy. Remove the focaccia from the pan to cool slightly or completely on a wire rack.

The Maillard reaction is that glorious process that happens when things like steak, marshmallows, and french fries are cooked and the reducing sugars react with amino acids. It's what gives bread that delicious golden-brown crust that everyone over the age of four loves. I don't think there's an instance where the Maillard reaction doesn't absolutely slap, but one of my favorites has got to be pretzels. Increasing the pH of the surface of any dough rapidly speeds up the reaction, leading to that signature deep golden brown of a pretzel.

Pretzel Focaccia with Beer Cheese

MAKES ONE 9-INCH SQUARE LOAF

FOR THE FOCACCIA

3¼ cups bread flour
2¼ teaspoons (1 packet) instant yeast
1½ teaspoons kosher salt
1 teaspoon sugar
1½ cups warm water
5 tablespoons olive oil, divided

FOR THE BEER CHEESE

1 cup cream cheese, room temperature
3–4 heaped tablespoons mayonnaise
1 tablespoon Dijon mustard
2 garlic cloves, minced
¼ cup light-flavored beer
1½–2 cups grated extra-old cheddar

FOR PRETZELING

¾ teaspoon baking soda
1 tablespoon hot tap water
1 egg yolk
Flaky salt or pretzel salt

For the focaccia, in a large bowl, stir the flour, yeast, salt, and sugar together. Make a well in the center. Add the warm water and 3 tablespoons of olive oil. Using a wooden spoon, stir for 1 to 2 minutes, until a stretchy, wet dough forms.

Grease a large clean bowl with 1 tablespoon of olive oil and transfer the dough to the bowl. Cover with a piece of plastic wrap or a dinner plate and set aside in a warm spot for 15 minutes.

After 15 minutes, dampen your hands and lift and stretch the dough onto itself a few times, working your way around the dough about two times and bringing the edges into the center. The dough should firm up a bit and be less sticky once you've done this turn. Flip the dough over so that it is seam side down, re-cover the bowl, and set aside in the warm spot for 30 minutes. Repeat the folding process one more time, then cover and set aside for 1 hour, or until the dough is doubled in size.

Grease a 9-inch square baking pan with nonstick cooking spray and add the remaining 1 tablespoon of oil. Lightly stretch the risen dough into the corners of the pan, being careful not to punch all the air out. Lightly cover the pan with a clean kitchen towel and set aside in the warm spot for 45 minutes to 1 hour, until puffy.

Meanwhile, preheat your oven to 425°F.

While the oven heats, make the beer cheese. In a medium bowl, beat the cream cheese, mayonnaise, Dijon, and garlic together. Beat in the beer and cheese, then transfer to a lightly greased 1-quart baking dish.

To pretzel the focaccia, whisk together the baking soda and hot water. Add the egg yolk and whisk to combine. Brush the mixture over the focaccia, then dampen your fingers and press them into the dough all the way through to the pan to dimple the surface. Scatter with flaky or pretzel salt.

Bake the focaccia alongside the beer cheese for 20 to 22 minutes, or until the focaccia is deeply golden and springy and the beer cheese is bubbling. Remove the focaccia from the pan and set on a wire rack. Let both the focaccia and the beer dip cool slightly before serving.

Baked Brie Focaccia
Focaccia Pizza

Pretzel Focaccia with Beer Cheese
Jelly Doughnut Focaccia

While calling this "focaccia pizza" is technically accurate, any fans of Motor City, Michigan, will recognize the inspiration behind this rectangular wonder. Detroit-style pizza is a glorious deep-dish polyhedron of thick, chewy crust not dissimilar to focaccia, wall-to-wall cheese with crispy edges, and a saucy top. For a Canadian twist and a bit of a nod to the city across the river, trying this recipe Windsor-style (i.e., with shredded pepperoni or salami) is a must.

Focaccia Pizza

MAKES ONE 9-BY-13-INCH PIZZA

FOR THE FOCACCIA BASE

3¼ cups bread flour

2¼ teaspoons (1 packet) instant yeast

1½ teaspoons kosher salt

1 teaspoon sugar

1½ cups warm water

6 tablespoons olive oil, divided

FOR THE PIZZA TOPPINGS

1¾ cups tomato passata or crushed tomatoes

2 garlic cloves, thinly sliced

1 tablespoon finely chopped fresh parsley

1 teaspoon dried Italian seasoning

½ teaspoon crushed red pepper flakes

Kosher salt

Freshly ground black pepper

12–14 oz brick mozzarella

2 oz pepperoni or hot Genoa salami, thinly sliced

For the focaccia, in a large bowl, combine the bread flour, yeast, salt, and sugar. Add the warm water and 3 tablespoons of olive oil. Using a wooden spoon, stir for 1 to 2 minutes, until a stretchy, wet dough forms.

Grease a large clean bowl with 1 tablespoon of olive oil and transfer the dough to the bowl. Cover with a piece of plastic wrap or a dinner plate and set aside in a warm spot for 15 minutes.

After 15 minutes, dampen your hands and lift and stretch the dough onto itself a few times, working your way around the dough about two times and bringing the edges into the center. The dough should firm up a bit and be less sticky once you've done this turn. Flip the dough over so that it is seam side down, re-cover the bowl, and set aside in the warm spot for 30 minutes. Repeat the folding process one more time, then cover and set aside for 1 hour, or until the dough is doubled in size.

Grease a 9-by-13-inch metal baking pan with the remaining 2 tablespoons of oil and transfer the dough into the pan. Lightly stretch the dough into the corners of the pan, being careful not to punch all the air out. Gently cover the pan with a clean kitchen towel and set aside in the warm spot for another 30 minutes.

Meanwhile, place your oven rack in the lowest position and preheat your oven to 500°F.

To prepare the sauce for the pizza, in a medium bowl, combine the tomato passata or crushed tomatoes, garlic, parsley, Italian seasoning, and red pepper flakes. Season with salt and pepper. Prepare the cheese by grating half the mozzarella and cutting the rest into ¼-inch cubes.

When the dough has risen, evenly scatter the grated cheese overtop, making sure to coat the whole crust right to the very edges. Scatter the cubed mozzarella overtop, again paying particular attention to the very edges of the crust, followed by the pepperoni or salami. Finally, dot the sauce over the cheese in a four-by-three grid (you can also spoon the sauce onto the pizza in three long lines—just don't cover the whole top with the sauce).

Bake the pizza for 16 to 18 minutes, or until the cheese has melted, is golden brown all over, and is super crispy around the edges, placing a sheet pan on the rack below in case of any cheesy boil-over. Allow the pizza to cool for about 5 minutes, then use a spatula to release the cheesy edges from the pan and transfer the pizza to a cutting board.

Note: The world is your oyster when it comes to toppings for this focaccia pizza, but for maximum deliciousness, add fresh toppings such as mushrooms, bell peppers, or onions directly onto the dough before the cheese. That will ensure they don't dry out in the heat of the oven.

I've never been a huge fan of baked doughnuts. They always feel more like circular cupcakes than doughy and delicious treats. While I have been known to bust out some hot oil to fry up a fresh batch of dodos at home, focaccia dough is the perfect baked stand-in thanks to all that olive oil. By adding the old-fashioned flavor of nutmeg to the dough itself, filling the dimples with your favorite jam, and dousing the finished product with a sweet vanilla glaze, you get all the flavors and textures of your favorite filled doughnut at home, without the fryer.

Jelly Doughnut Focaccia

MAKES ONE 9-INCH SQUARE LOAF

FOR THE DOUGHNUTS

3¼ cups bread flour

2¼ teaspoons (1 packet) instant yeast

1½ teaspoons kosher salt

1 teaspoon sugar

½ teaspoon freshly grated nutmeg

1½ cups warm water

5 tablespoons olive oil, divided

½–¾ cup strawberry, raspberry, or cherry jam

FOR THE GLAZE

1 cup icing sugar

2–3 tablespoons milk or cream

½ teaspoon vanilla extract

For the doughnuts, in a large bowl, combine the bread flour, yeast, salt, sugar, and nutmeg. Make a well in the center. Add the warm water and 3 tablespoons of olive oil. Using a wooden spoon, stir for 1 to 2 minutes, until a stretchy, wet dough forms.

Grease a large clean bowl with 1 tablespoon of olive oil and transfer the dough to the bowl. Cover with a piece of plastic wrap or a dinner plate and set aside in a warm spot for 15 minutes.

After 15 minutes, dampen your hands and lift and stretch the dough onto itself a few times, working your way around the dough about two times and bringing the edges into the center. The dough should firm up a bit and be less sticky once you've done this turn. Flip the dough over so that it is seam side down, re-cover the bowl, and set aside in the warm spot for 30 minutes. Repeat the folding process one more time, then cover and set aside for 1 hour, or until the dough is doubled in size.

Add the remaining 1 tablespoon of oil to a 9-inch square baking pan and transfer the dough to the pan. Lightly stretch the dough into the corners of the pan, being careful not to punch all the air out. Gently cover the pan with a clean kitchen towel and set aside in the warm spot for 45 minutes to 1 hour, until puffy.

Preheat your oven to 425°F. Dampen your fingers with water or a little oil and press into the dough all the way through to the pan to dimple the surface. Dollop the jam over the dimples in the focaccia.

Bake for 20 to 22 minutes, or until golden and springy. Remove the focaccia from the pan to cool slightly on a wire rack.

Meanwhile, prepare the glaze. In a small bowl, whisk together the icing sugar, milk or cream, and vanilla, adding more milk or cream to reach a pourable consistency.

Drizzle the glaze over the warm focaccia and set aside to cool slightly or completely to room temperature before serving.

Every season has its own particular brand of nostalgia. Where fall is all sharpened pencils and crunchy leaves, winter is dark nights and shimmering snow, spring is burgeoning bright green and birds chirping, and summer—for me—is wet bathing suits and malt vinegar. In the Berg house, summer is not complete without a trip to Shelby's Chipwagon in Gravenhurst, Ontario, where my family has relaxed by the lake for generations. While those fries are most definitely triple-cooked to deep golden-brown perfection, I personally don't have time for that when the craving strikes at home. With this recipe, there's no soaking, no blanching, and no triple-cooking. Just chip-truck-worthy fries in a flash.

The Cool Guy Fry

SERVES 4 TO 6

4 medium russet potatoes
Canola oil
Kosher salt

Scrub and dry the potatoes, then cut into ¼-inch-thick fries. Add the fries to a large Dutch oven and pour in enough oil to cover the fries by about ¼ inch.

Cover the pot with a lid, place over high heat, and bring to a boil. This should take about 5 to 7 minutes. Once boiling, remove the lid and fry the potatoes, without stirring, for 10 minutes.

After 10 minutes, carefully stir the potatoes, being sure to release any fries that have stuck to the bottom of the pan. Continue to fry the potatoes for 10 more minutes, or until deeply golden and crisp.

Prepare a landing zone for your fries by lining a sheet pan with a cooling rack. Once the fries are golden, use a slotted spoon or a pair of tongs to carefully transfer the fries to the lined pan. Season immediately with salt and allow to cool slightly.

The fries are best served right away, but if needed, keep the fries warm in a 200°F oven until ready to serve.

Note: This cold oil method for making french fries takes a page out of the boiled potato playbook. To cook these incredibly dense little tubers, you often start them in cold water (or, in this case, oil) and then bring them up to a boil. That allows potatoes to cook more gradually and evenly rather than over-cooking the outside and undercooking the center.

I feel like my mom's most brilliant culinary instinct is to add some sort of crunchy topping to any and every starch. From her classic mac and cheese to these perfect potatoes that grace every Berg family holiday table, the combination of butter, cheese, and a bit of crunch courtesy of the cracker or cereal aisle at the grocery store just feels like home to me.

Myra's Mashed Potato Casserole

SERVES 8

- 5 lb yellow potatoes, peeled and quartered
- Kosher salt
- ⅓ cup + 2 tablespoons butter, divided
- 1 cup brick-style cream cheese, cubed
- 1 cup sour cream
- 2 cups grated medium cheddar
- 2 cups crushed cornflakes

Preheat your oven to 350°F. Lightly grease a 3-quart casserole dish with nonstick cooking spray.

Place the potatoes in a large pot and cover with cold tap water. Season well with salt, cover the pot with a slightly off-kilter lid, and bring to a boil over high heat. Cook the potatoes until fork tender, 15 to 20 minutes.

Drain the potatoes well and return to the pot. Add ⅓ cup of butter along with the cream cheese and sour cream and beat with a hand mixer on medium speed just until smooth. Season well with salt and transfer to the prepared casserole dish.

Scatter the top with most of the cheese followed by the cornflakes. Top with the remaining cheese and dot with the remaining 2 tablespoons of butter.

Bake the casserole for 30 to 35 minutes, or until the edges are golden brown and the center is piping hot.

Note: You can prepare this casserole up to 3 days in advance. Simply cover the unbaked casserole with plastic wrap and store in the fridge. Add 15 to 20 minutes to the baking time to ensure the center is warm.

There are exactly zero things that I find more comforting than watching any rendition of Jane Austen's *Pride and Prejudice*. The BBC miniseries is obviously canon and the freeze-frames at the end of every episode give me life (also, Colin Firth's Darcy diving into that pond?! Hubba hubba!). But for me as a millennial, the 2005 Keira Knightley version is clearly cinematic perfection. As soon as I hear the music, my shoulders drop. At the hand flex, I legit giggle. And when the Bennets' doorstep is darkened by one Mr. Collins, my eyes never stop rolling. With this recipe, you'll realize that it has been years since you had such an exemplary vegetable.

What Excellent Boiled Potatoes

SERVES 4

1½ lb yellow potatoes
Kosher salt
7 oz soft feta (see note)
1 garlic clove, minced
1 lemon, zested and juiced
1 tablespoon grainy Dijon mustard
¾ cup plain Greek yogurt or sour cream
2–3 tablespoons butter
¼ cup chopped fresh parsley, dill, and/or chives

Peel and halve or quarter the potatoes. Place in a large pot and cover with cold tap water. Season well with salt and bring to a boil over medium-high heat. Boil until fork tender, about 15 minutes, then drain and set aside to steam dry.

Meanwhile, crumble the feta into the bowl of your food processor and add the garlic, lemon zest, and lemon juice. Process until well combined, scraping down the sides of the bowl as needed. Add the mustard and Greek yogurt or sour cream and blitz until creamy. Set aside.

Once the potatoes are dry but still hot, transfer the potatoes back to the pot and add the butter and herbs. Cover the pot to allow the butter to melt, then season with salt and toss well to evenly coat the potatoes in the melted butter and herbs.

Transfer the whipped feta to a large serving dish and spread into an even bed for the potatoes. Spoon the potatoes overtop and serve.

Note: When buying soft feta, look for a variety that contains sheep's milk. It will be softer and creamier, making for a smoother whipped feta.

This recipe is a bit of a throwback to Grade 6 science, when my mind was first blown by the wonders of the pH scale. By boiling the potatoes in baking soda–spiked water, you're not only releasing extra starch but also slightly increasing the pH of the surface of the potatoes, leading to a more intense Maillard reaction and therefore a more intense golden-brown crunch. With this little trick, you too can have the crispiest-on-the-outside, fluffiest-on-the-inside, most golden-brown potatoes ever.

The Crispiest Roast Potatoes

SERVES 4

2¼ lb yellow potatoes
2 teaspoons baking soda
Kosher salt
5 tablespoons olive oil, divided
4 garlic cloves, skin on
Freshly ground black pepper
2 sprigs fresh sage or rosemary
½ lemon, zested
Sour cream, for serving

Preheat your oven to 450°F and set the rack in the lowest position.

Quarter the potatoes, place in a large pot, and and add enough cold tap water to cover by 1 inch. Stir in the baking soda, season heavily with salt, and bring to a boil over high heat. Parboil the potatoes just until slightly fork tender, 10 to 12 minutes, then drain and allow to completely air-dry.

Coat the bottom of a large sheet pan with 1 tablespoon of oil and place on the bottom rack of the oven to heat for about 5 minutes.

Lightly crush the garlic cloves just to burst the skin and transfer to a large mixing bowl. Add the potatoes and remaining 4 tablespoons of oil. Season with salt and pepper and, using a rubber spatula or wooden spoon, gently toss the potatoes for about 1 minute to develop some of the potato starches. The potatoes will start to look a little fluffy around the edges—that's exactly what you're aiming for.

Carefully remove the sheet pan from the oven and add the potatoes in a single layer. Roast for 25 minutes, or until the underside of the potatoes is a deep golden brown. Meanwhile, drizzle a little oil onto the herbs. Flip the potatoes over, add the herbs to the pan, and continue to roast for 10 to 15 minutes, or until crisp and golden.

Remove the potatoes from the oven, immediately grate the lemon zest overtop, and season with more salt and pepper. Transfer to a serving dish and serve with sour cream on the side.

If you've ever wondered what would happen if mashed potatoes had a baby with cheese fondue, allow me to introduce you to pommes aligot. It's essentially a mixture of two parts potato to one part grated cheese, and this ultra creamy, super cheesy, way-too-delicious concoction takes its already delicious beginnings and makes something truly incredible. It's a cinch to throw together, but do your future self a favor and immediately rinse your utensils and pot when you're finished with them. Mashed or riced potatoes tend to turn into concrete and become darn near impossible to scrape off.

Pommes Aligot

SERVES 4

1 lb russet potatoes
3 garlic cloves, peeled
Kosher salt
½ cup butter, melted
½ cup buttermilk
8 oz Gruyère or Comté, grated
Freshly grated nutmeg

Peel the potatoes and cut into a large dice. Place in a pot and top with cold tap water. Add the garlic cloves and season well with salt.

Bring to a boil over medium-high heat and cook until the potatoes are very tender, about 15 minutes. Drain the potatoes and garlic, then pass them through a ricer or press through a fine-mesh sieve. Transfer the potatoes back to the pot.

Stir in the butter and buttermilk and place the pot over medium-low heat. Gradually stir in the cheese and continue to stir until the potatoes are smooth and the cheese is stringy. Season well with salt and a pinch of nutmeg.

Serve immediately or cover and keep warm over low heat until ready to serve.

Note: If you have any grated mozzarella hanging around, feel free to add a handful or two to the potatoes for extra stringy cheesiness.

Veggin' Out

I'm here to convince you that vegetables can (and should!) be indulgent and totally comforting additions to your table.

Back in the '90s and early 2000s, a certain brand of salad dressing carried a tasty bottled Caesar-ish dressing known as Golden Caesar. Sure, the name referred to the fact that this dressing was a golden vinaigrette rather than the creamy dip-ish situation that most store-bought Caesars tend to be, but I'd argue that it also represented its high-standing flavor rank. This was one of two dressings that the Berg family used during my formative years, so let's throw it back and whip up an ode to the golden king!

Shredded Kale Salad with Crispies

SERVES 4

1 lemon
¼ small red onion, thinly sliced
1 garlic clove, minced
1 anchovy fillet, minced
Kosher salt
Freshly ground black pepper
5–6 tablespoons olive oil, divided
2–3 tablespoons ground Parmigiano-Reggiano, plus more for serving
1 large bunch Tuscan kale
1 tablespoon capers
¼ cup panko breadcrumbs

Using a vegetable peeler, remove the lemon zest from the lemon and thinly slice into short strips. Alternatively, you can just zest the lemon with a rasp, but I like the bigger pieces in this salad. Set half of the lemon zest aside and add the rest to a large bowl. Juice in the lemon, then add the sliced onions, garlic, and anchovies. Season with salt and lots of pepper and whisk to combine.

While still whisking, slowly drizzle in 4 or 5 tablespoons of olive oil, then stir in the Parmigiano-Reggiano.

Remove the stems from the kale and thinly slice the leaves. Add the leaves to the bowl and set aside.

Add the remaining 1 tablespoon of oil to a small skillet over medium-high heat. While the oil heats, dry the capers very well with some paper towel. Carefully add the capers to the hot oil and fry for 30 seconds to 1 minute, or until slightly golden and shriveled. Use a slotted spoon to transfer the capers to a small bowl and set aside.

Add the panko and remaining lemon zest to the hot oil and toast just until the panko is golden, 1 to 2 minutes. Add the panko to the capers and set aside to cool slightly.

When ready to serve, toss the salad well and scatter with the crispy topping and some extra Parm and pepper.

Note: For pure Mary Berg in Grade 6 energy, toss some cooked shrimp on there and call it lunch.

For a vegetarian version, swap the chicken with extra firm tofu and the bacon with roughly chopped smoked almonds.

Not to exaggerate or anything, but my mom, Myra, is probably the world's number-one fan of salads. I cannot tell you the hours we've spent on road trips blasting by off-ramps as tummies grumble with hunger, because this or that restaurant with her favorite salad of the moment isn't listed on the roadside sign. Even at home, I can spend the day cooking up a veritable feast only to have her *exclusively* rave about the boring old salad I threw together at the last minute. In order for everyone to win, a hearty salad like this rightfully does steal the show and keeps everyone in the Berg household very happy (me, because my culinary efforts are guaranteed to be noticed in salad form; Myra, because salad).

Classic Cobb Salad with Maple Chipotle Chicken

SERVES 4 TO 6

FOR THE CHICKEN & BACON

⅓ cup chipotle peppers in adobo sauce (see note)

2 garlic cloves, roughly chopped

3 tablespoons maple syrup

½ lemon, zested and juiced

1½ teaspoons ground cumin

Olive oil

Kosher salt

Freshly ground black pepper

4–6 boneless, skinless chicken thighs

6 slices bacon

FOR THE SALAD

3–4 eggs

1 head leaf lettuce, torn or chopped

1 pint cherry tomatoes, halved

1 avocado, cut into cubes

4½ oz blue cheese, crumbled

3 tablespoons chopped fresh chives

For the chicken, in a small food processor, blitz the chipotle peppers in adobo, garlic, maple syrup, lemon zest, lemon juice, and cumin until smooth. Add about 1 tablespoon of oil and season with salt and pepper. Place the chicken thighs in a baking dish or zip-top bag, pour the marinade overtop, and set aside at room temperature for 15 minutes or, for a longer marinade, cover and refrigerate for up to 8 hours.

When ready to cook, line a sheet pan with parchment paper and lay out the bacon in a single layer. Add the bacon to your cold oven, then heat it to 425°F. When the oven reaches temperature, set a timer for 6 minutes. When the time is up, the bacon should be golden and crisp. If not, continue to cook the bacon for a few minutes, keeping an eye on it to make sure it doesn't burn. Once crisp, transfer the bacon to a paper towel–lined plate and set aside.

Remove the chicken thighs from the marinade, add to the bacon pan, and return to the oven to bake for 25 minutes, or until cooked through to 165°F. Set aside to rest for 5 minutes.

Meanwhile, for the salad, bring a small pot of water to a boil over high heat. Once boiling, carefully lower in the eggs and cook for 7 minutes for a jammy yolk or 10 minutes for a hard yolk. Immediately drain the eggs and rinse under cold water until cool enough to handle. Peel the eggs and set aside.

Arrange the lettuce on a large serving platter. Chop the bacon and halve the eggs and arrange overtop, then add the tomatoes, avocados, blue cheese, and chives. Slice the chicken and arrange on top.

CONTINUED

FOR THE DRESSING

3 tablespoons apple cider vinegar
1 tablespoon lemon juice
1 garlic clove, minced
1 tablespoon Dijon mustard
1 tablespoon maple syrup
¼ cup olive oil
Kosher salt
Freshly ground black pepper

For the dressing, in a small bowl, whisk together the vinegar, lemon juice, and garlic. Whisk in the mustard and maple syrup, then slowly drizzle in the oil while whisking to emulsify and bring everything together. Season to taste with salt and pepper. Lightly dress the salad and season with salt and pepper.

Serve immediately with the remaining dressing on the side.

Note: A can of chipotle peppers in adobo sauce is a great flavor booster to keep on hand, but lots of recipes, like this one, don't use the whole can. For easy storage of any remaining peppers, just blitz everything up in a small food processor and transfer to a zip-top bag. Flatten the bag and store in the freezer for up to 3 months. When you find yourself looking for a spicy or smoky something, just break off a little piece of the frozen puree and add it to whatever you're making.

Savory or sweet, galettes are the easiest pies to make. To keep things extra breezy and avoid a mess, you might be tempted to roll out the pastry on a sheet of parchment paper, but please learn from my mistake and don't do that! While parchment is nonstick for baking, the raw dough will stick to the paper as you roll it out, making it more difficult to get a thin, even sheet of pastry. It will also require you to work the dough more, leading to increased gluten development and a tough pastry. While a little messy, a good old-fashioned dusting of flour is all you need.

Potato Leek Galette

SERVES 8

FOR THE PASTRY

1 cup all-purpose flour

1 cup whole wheat flour

1 teaspoon kosher salt

¼ teaspoon freshly ground black pepper

1 cup cold butter, cut into small cubes

½ cup coarsely grated Parmigiano-Reggiano

1 egg

¼ cup milk

FOR THE FILLING

1 lb (about 2 medium) yellow potatoes

2 mild or spicy Italian sausages

3 garlic cloves, skin on

1 teaspoon curry powder

Kosher salt

Freshly ground black pepper

Olive oil

2–3 leeks, thinly sliced and washed (see note)

Grated nutmeg

1 cup ricotta

1 cup finely grated Parmigiano-Reggiano

For the pastry, in a large bowl, combine the flours, salt, and pepper. Add the butter and, using your fingertips, pinch and snap the butter into the flour mixture until it resembles coarse crumbs and the butter pieces are no larger than a pea. Add the cheese, tossing to mix.

In a small bowl, whisk the egg and milk together, then add to the flour mixture and stir just until combined and the dough holds together when squeezed in your palm. Turn the pastry out and knead a few times to bring together. Wrap in plastic wrap and refrigerate for at least 1 hour or up to 1 day.

Place your oven rack in the lowest position and preheat the oven to 425°F.

For the filling, slice the potatoes into about ¼-inch-thick rounds and transfer to a sheet pan. Using the tip of a sharp knife, split the sausage casings open and remove the meat. Discard the casings and roughly tear the meat into small chunks. Add the meat to the sheet pan along with the garlic cloves, season with the curry powder, salt, and pepper, and drizzle with about 1 tablespoon of oil. Toss well to combine, then roast for 15 to 18 minutes, just until the potatoes and garlic are tender and the sausage has picked up a little color. Set aside to cool.

Meanwhile, place a sauté pan or skillet over medium heat and add a little oil. Add the leeks, season with salt, pepper, and a pinch of nutmeg, and cover the pan with a lid. Cook the leeks down for 5 to 10 minutes, or until softened and slightly jammy, stirring occasionally. Set aside to cool.

Retrieve the roasted garlic from the cooled potatoes, remove their skins, and add the cloves to a bowl. Mash with a fork or the back of a spoon, then stir in the ricotta, grated Parmigiano-Reggiano, Dijon, and herbs. Season with kosher salt, pepper, and a pinch of nutmeg.

CONTINUED

2 tablespoons Dijon mustard

2 teaspoons finely chopped fresh sage or ½ teaspoon dried herb blend

1 egg

1 tablespoon water or milk

Flaky salt, optional

On a well-floured surface, roll out the pastry to about ¼ inch thick, then transfer to a sheet of parchment paper. Spread the ricotta mixture over the pastry, leaving about a 2-inch border all the way around. Top with the potatoes and sausage, then spread the leeks overtop. Fold the edges of the pastry up and over some of the filling to form a crust, then transfer along with the parchment paper, to a sheet pan.

Beat the egg with the water or milk to make an egg wash and brush over the crust. Scatter with flaky salt, if using, and bake for 35 to 40 minutes, or until golden and crisp.

Note: Leeks always need a good wash. To clean them, place sliced leeks in a large bowl and cover with tap water. Run your hands through the leeks, agitating them so that any dirt and sand falls away to the bottom of the bowl. Using your hands, scoop the leeks out of the water, allowing as much water as possible to drain away, then set aside or add to the pan to cook.

Roasted vegetables might not immediately come to mind when thinking of comfort food, but I've always had a soft spot for the caramelized deliciousness of a sheet pan of tender veg. For those in doubt, I've found that adding the flavors of Caesar salad to pretty much anything can convince even the staunchest skeptic.

Caesar Roasted Veg

SERVES 4 TO 6

FOR THE VEG

Olive oil

Kosher salt

1 bunch broccolini or 1 head broccoli, cut into florets

1 bunch asparagus

2 garlic cloves, minced

½ lemon, zested and juiced

2 teaspoons Dijon mustard

Freshly ground black pepper

½ cup finely grated Parmigiano-Reggiano

FOR THE CRUNCH

2 tablespoons olive oil

1 garlic clove, minced

½ cup panko breadcrumbs (see note)

Kosher salt

Freshly ground black pepper

½ lemon, zested

¼ cup finely grated Parmigiano-Reggiano

For the veg, bring a large pot of water to a boil and preheat your oven to 425°F. Line a sheet pan with parchment paper, drizzle it with a little olive oil, and set aside.

Season the water very well with salt, add the broccolini or broccoli, and blanch just until bright green and the stems are slightly tender, 2 to 3 minutes. Drain and allow it to steam dry.

Meanwhile, trim or snap off the woody ends of the asparagus and set the tender stalks aside.

In a large bowl, whisk the garlic, lemon zest, lemon juice, and Dijon with 2 to 3 tablespoons of olive oil. Add the asparagus and broccoli, season with salt and pepper, and toss well to combine and evenly coat the veg with the oil mixture.

Scatter the sheet pan with the grated Parmigiano-Reggiano and arrange the veg overtop in one layer. Roast for 12 to 15 minutes, or until lightly charred and the veg is a bit frizzly on the ends.

Meanwhile, for the crunch, add the oil to a medium skillet over medium heat. Stir in the garlic and panko, season with salt and pepper, and toast, stirring often, until golden brown. Stir in the lemon zest and transfer to a dish to cool slightly before tossing with the Parmigiano-Reggiano.

Using a spatula, lift the veg and crispy cheese crust from the parchment paper and transfer to a serving dish. Scatter with the crunch and season with more pepper, if desired.

Note: If you don't have panko on hand, you can substitute it with a slice or two of stale bread. Blitz the bread in your food processor or tear it into small crumbs and toast in the pan as you would the panko.

Back when I was studying at the University of Toronto, at least once a week you'd find me at the iconic Sneaky Dee's at the corner of College and Bathurst, splitting a pitcher of cheap beer and scarfing down a mountain of fully-loaded 'chos. To relive those nights without my shoes sticking to a dive bar floor and with the added benefit of, you know, nutrients, I've swapped out the soggy tortilla chips for seasoned roasted veg.

Nachos for Dinner

SERVES 4

FOR THE NACHOS

- 2 medium sweet potatoes, scrubbed or peeled
- 1 head cauliflower
- 2 small red onions
- 3 tablespoons olive oil
- 2 teaspoons chili powder
- 1 teaspoon ground cumin
- 1 teaspoon garlic powder
- 1 teaspoon smoked paprika
- ½ teaspoon dried oregano
- ½ teaspoon onion powder
- Kosher salt
- 1 can (19 fl oz) black beans, drained and rinsed
- 1½–2 cups grated nacho cheese blend

FOR SERVING

- ¾ cup crumbled feta
- 1 avocado, diced, and/or guacamole
- 2 green onions, thinly sliced
- Pickled jalapeños
- Cilantro
- Prepared salsa
- Plain Greek yogurt or skyr
- Lime wedges
- Hot sauce

Preheat your oven to 425°F.

Halve the sweet potatoes and cut each half into four to six wedges. Cut the cauliflower into florets and the red onions into eight wedges each. Transfer the veg to a large sheet pan and drizzle with the olive oil. In a small bowl, combine the chili powder, cumin, garlic powder, smoked paprika, oregano, and onion powder, then sprinkle over the vegetables. Season with salt and toss to combine and coat the veg with the oil and seasoning.

Spread the vegetables in an even layer and roast for 25 minutes. At this point, add the black beans to the sheet pan and give everything a stir. Return the veg to the oven and continue to roast for another 10 to 15 minutes, or until the veg are tender and golden and the black beans have begun to split and crisp up.

Scatter the grated cheese overtop and return to the oven for another 5 to 10 minutes, or until the cheese is melted and lightly golden.

Serve immediately topped with feta, avocado and/or guacamole, green onions, and pickled jalapeños and cilantro, to taste. Serve with bowls of salsa and yogurt or skyr on the side, as well as a few lime wedges and hot sauce.

A few years back, Aaron and I found a holiday house in the hills of Tuscany that feels like a little slice of heaven. There is everything we could ever want there: a great little kitchen for cooking up everything that pops into my head, a cat named Peggy who is as old as the sun, and rosemary and sage bushes roughly the size of a small bus. The first thing we do when we arrive in our little town is hit up the local grocery store for a few hours to fill my cart. With a mixture of staples and impulse buys, I know I've got fixings for at least a few days, but nearing the end of the week, meals become what we call "use-em-ups." This little number was thanks to Thursday's aperitivo, Wednesday's pasta sauce, and a quick little pantry raid. It's a one-pot dish reminiscent of the ever-amazing Smitten Kitchen's pizza beans and is the most glorious way to polish off a stack of leftovers.

Cheesy Beans

SERVES 4

- 1½ oz spicy genoa or fennel salami
- 1 tablespoon olive oil
- 1 small yellow or red onion, diced
- Kosher salt
- Freshly ground black pepper
- 2 garlic cloves, thinly sliced
- 1½ teaspoons dried Italian seasoning
- ¼–½ teaspoon crushed red pepper flakes
- 2 cans (19 fl oz each) cannellini beans, drained and rinsed
- 1 can (26 fl oz) crushed tomatoes (see note)
- 2–3 handfuls dark, leafy greens, roughly chopped
- 2 tablespoons prepared basil pesto
- 2½ cups grated mozzarella
- Crusty bread or flatbread, for serving

Place a cast-iron or oven-safe skillet over medium heat.

Dice or thinly slice the salami. Add it to the pan and cook until crisp, stirring often, about 2 minutes. Remove the crispy salami from the pan and set aside.

Add the oil and onions to the pan, season with salt and pepper, and cook until softened and lightly golden brown, about 5 minutes. Stir in the garlic, Italian seasoning, and red pepper flakes and continue to cook for 30 seconds.

Add the beans to the pan and cook for 3 to 4 minutes, or until they pick up a little color and the skins are just starting to burst. Carefully add the canned tomatoes and place an off-kilter lid over the pan to avoid splatter. Simmer for 5 minutes to bring the flavors together, then stir in the greens and continue to cook for 2 to 3 minutes to wilt.

Remove the pan from the heat and stir in the pesto. Scatter the grated cheese and crispy salami overtop and transfer to the center rack of your oven. Turn the broiler to high and broil for 5 minutes, or until the cheese is melted and lightly golden brown.

Serve immediately alongside some crusty bread or flatbread.

Note: For more texture, substitute the crushed tomatoes for 2 cans (14 fl oz each) of cherry tomatoes.

Two of the most universal categories in the world of comfort food are creamy things and fried things. Depending on which you're craving, this recipe lets you have it either way. Whether fried to a crisp or soft and stodgy, polenta is the perfect base for almost any topping, but these cheesy mushrooms are a delight.

Creamy Mushrooms with Polenta

SERVES 4 (AS A MAIN, MORE AS A CRISPY FRIED SNACK)

FOR THE POLENTA

- 3 cups vegetable or chicken broth (page 45 or store-bought)
- 1 cup milk
- 2 garlic cloves, minced
- 1 cup yellow cornmeal
- ½ cup finely grated Parmigiano-Reggiano
- 2 tablespoons butter
- Kosher salt
- Freshly ground black pepper

FOR THE MUSHROOMS

- 8 oz mixed mushrooms, roughly chopped or torn
- Kosher salt
- Freshly ground black pepper
- 2 tablespoons butter
- 2 garlic cloves, finely minced
- ½ cup dry white wine
- ½ cup cream
- ¼–½ cup finely grated Parmigiano-Reggiano
- 2 tablespoons chopped fresh parsley or dill

For the polenta, in a medium pot with a tight-fitting lid, bring the broth and milk to a boil over high heat. Stir in the garlic, then slowly whisk in the cornmeal. When the cornmeal has thickened slightly, cover the pot with the lid, turn the heat down to low, and simmer until thickened and creamy, 25 to 30 minutes, stirring every 5 minutes or so. Whisk in the cheese and butter and season with salt and pepper. Keep the polenta covered and hold over very low heat, stirring occasionally. If serving the polenta crispy, you'll need to cook the polenta the day before (see note).

For the mushrooms, place a large sauté pan over medium heat. Add the mushrooms to the dry hot pan, season with salt and pepper, and cook, stirring often, until slightly cooked down and starting to color around the edges, about 5 minutes.

Add the butter and garlic and cook for 30 seconds to 1 minute. Deglaze the pan with the wine and allow it to reduce by about half. Pour in the cream and bring to a simmer, then whisk in the cheese and season to taste with more salt and pepper.

To serve, divide the polenta into bowls and spoon the creamy mushrooms overtop. Garnish with some herbs and enjoy immediately.

Note: For crispy polenta, transfer the cooked polenta to a lightly greased loaf or baking pan, set aside to cool to room temperature, then cover and transfer to the fridge to chill overnight. Slice into your desired portions and pan-fry in a little oil over medium-high heat until golden, crisp, and heated through, 6 to 8 minutes per side. Spoon the creamy mushrooms over the fried polenta and garnish with the herbs.

Pasta Please

Cheesy, saucy, stuffed, or baked, the pasta-bilities are endless.

Please don't be mad at me for that *excellent* dad joke or for the fact that there are two risotto recipes in this chapter.

I'm ashamed to say that there was a time in my life when I thought I had to grow beyond certain homey, comforting, and delicious dishes. I felt that to prove I was a good cook, I had to embody this culinary-bro attitude and shirk foods that are made simply and without pretense. So I lived a few years of my life tuna-pasta-salad-less, and let me tell you, they were bleak times. I'm happy to say that I am no longer a wannabe jabroni, and now I live my life with a real "not gonna yuck anyone's yum" (including my own) mentality.

Updated Tuna Pasta Salad

SERVES 6 TO 8

½ red onion, thinly sliced
½ cup red wine vinegar
1 teaspoon sugar
Kosher salt
Freshly ground black pepper
½ fennel bulb, thinly sliced and fronds reserved
1 lemon, zested and juiced
10½ oz rotini or radiatori pasta
½ cup mayonnaise
2–3 tablespoons prepared pesto
2 teaspoons Dijon mustard
7 oz jarred or canned tuna
1 can (19 fl oz) chickpeas, drained and rinsed
2 cups chopped radicchio
¼ cup chopped fresh parsley
1 small handful fresh basil leaves

In a small bowl or jar, stir together the onions, red wine vinegar, and sugar and season well with salt and pepper. Set aside to pickle for at least 20 minutes, or cover and let pickle in the fridge for a few hours or up to 2 weeks.

Place the sliced fennel in a large bowl, reserving the fronds for later, and toss with the lemon zest and juice. Set aside.

Bring a large pot of water to a boil over high heat. Season well with salt and cook the pasta according to the package directions. Strain and rinse the pasta with cold water (see note). Set aside to drain and cool completely.

Add the mayonnaise, pesto, and mustard to the bowl with the fennel. Scoop about 2 tablespoons of the onion pickling liquid into the bowl and whisk to combine. Season to taste with salt and pepper.

Add the pasta and pickled onions to the bowl, leaving the rest of the pickling liquid behind. (Reserve this pickling liquid to add to salad dressings, or simply add some more sliced onions to the mix so that you have more pickled onions on hand for future recipes.) Add the tuna and chickpeas to the bowl and toss well to mix.

Gently stir in the radicchio, parsley, basil, and fennel fronds and season with a bit more salt and pepper, if needed.

Serve immediately or store in the fridge for up to 2 days.

Note: Rinsing pasta is typically a no-no, as that lovely starch on the noodles helps sauces stick. But for pasta salad, a quick rinse not only cools the noodles faster but also keeps the pasta salad from turning into a starchy block in the fridge.

Everyone needs a basic risotto recipe, and for me, this is it. With a mixture of both pecorino Romano and Parmigiano-Reggiano and lots of freshly ground black pepper, the familiar flavors of cacio e pepe are perfect as they are, but they also make a perfect base for any mix-ins your heart desires or your fridge requires (i.e., any bits and bobs that need to be eaten up).

Cacio e Pepe Risotto

SERVES 4

- 1½ tablespoons olive oil
- 2 shallots, finely diced
- Kosher salt
- 1 cup arborio rice
- ½ cup dry white wine
- 2½ cups chicken or vegetable broth (page 45 or store-bought), warmed
- ⅔ cup finely grated pecorino Romano
- ⅓ cup finely grated Parmigiano-Reggiano
- Freshly ground black pepper

Set a large sauté pan over medium heat and add the oil. Add the shallots, season with salt, and cook just until translucent and lightly golden around the edges, 2 to 3 minutes. Add the arborio rice and cook for 1 minute, stirring often to toast the rice.

Turn the heat down to medium-low and add the white wine. Stir until almost all the wine has been absorbed, then start adding the warm broth about ½ cup at a time, stirring well after each addition and leaving it to bubble away until absorbed before adding and stirring in the next ½ cup of broth.

Once the rice is tender, stir in the pecorino and Parmigiano, season to taste with salt and lots of black pepper, and add a bit more broth to loosen, if needed. Serve immediately.

Note: Just before serving your risotto, you might need to add another splash of broth to reach the right consistency. You're looking for the risotto to almost act like a wave when tossing it in the pan.

Golden brown is widely considered to be the most delicious color. I mean, think about it. There's caramel, brown butter, roast chicken, french fries . . . I could go on. But just because something is clearly screaming that it's chockablock full of vitamins doesn't mean it can't be creamy, dreamy, and totally craveable.

Get Your Greens Risotto

SERVES 4

- 4½ cups vegetable or chicken broth (page 45 or store-bought)
- 1 cup broccoli florets, frozen or fresh
- 3½–5 oz kale or spinach, frozen or fresh
- 3 tablespoons butter
- 1 yellow onion, finely chopped
- Kosher salt
- Freshly ground black pepper
- 2 garlic cloves
- 1½ cups arborio rice
- ½ cup dry white wine
- 1 cup frozen peas
- 2 tablespoons prepared pesto
- 1 lemon, zested and juiced
- ½ cup finely grated pecorino Romano or Parmigiano-Reggiano

In a large saucepan, bring the broth to a boil over high heat. Add the broccoli and cook for 2 minutes if frozen, 5 minutes if fresh, or until tender. Add the kale or spinach and continue to cook for 1 minute whether frozen or fresh, just until the greens are tender but still bright. Using a slotted spoon, remove the broccoli and greens from the hot broth and transfer to your blender. Add about ½ cup of the broth, loosen the vent cap of your blender, blitz until smooth, then set aside. Remove the broth from the heat.

In a large sauté pan or saucepan over medium heat, melt the butter. Add the onions, season with salt and pepper, and cook until softened, about 5 minutes. Add the garlic and arborio rice and toast for 1 to 2 minutes.

Stir in the white wine and cook until the wine is absorbed. Using a ladle, add about ½ cup of the hot broth to the rice and stir to combine. Stir the rice often until the broth is absorbed, then add another ladleful. Continue adding broth in this manner until the rice is cooked to al dente.

Stir the pureed greens and frozen peas into the risotto and continue to cook until thickened, 3 to 5 minutes. If the risotto is a little on the thick side, add a splash of broth or water.

Just before serving, stir in the pesto, lemon zest, lemon juice, and cheese and season to taste with more salt and pepper, if needed.

Note: For a golden-brown switch-up to this risotto, use leftovers to make crispy fried Arancini (page 75).

Slightly Grown-Up Stovetop Mac 136
Caprese Mac & Cheese 138
Charcuterie Board Mac & Cheese 139

Mac & Cheese 5 Ways

The quintessence of cozy, there is no way to talk about comfort food and not talk about mac and cheese. Eaten straight from the pot or baked up to golden-brown perfection, it's basically the food version of your favorite sweatshirt.

Isn't it just the best when you're hanging out with your buds and, even after knowing each other for a while, they teach you something new?! That's one of my favorite things about spending time with my foodie friends. We get together, nerd out over new flavor combinations, jars of jam, mustards, and anything else we're currently pumped about, and share new tips, tricks, and techniques we've picked up along the way. I've always been a fan of mac and cheese in general, but I have a special place in my heart (and belly) for the classic boxed stuff. This recipe was one I'd been tinkering with for a while, and it had been an extra cheesy week at work (literally) when Andrea Buckett and Anna Olson came in to share recipes. It is to them that I dedicate the genius additions of cornstarch and turmeric to this now-perfected pot of cheesy goodness.

Slightly Grown-Up Stovetop Mac

SERVES 4 TO 6

- Kosher salt
- 2 cups elbow macaroni
- 1 cup cottage cheese
- 2 tablespoons butter
- 2 garlic cloves, minced
- 1 cup milk
- 1 tablespoon cornstarch
- ½ teaspoon mustard powder
- ¼ teaspoon ground turmeric
- ¼ teaspoon onion powder
- 2 cups grated extra-old orange cheddar

Bring a pot of water to a boil and season well with salt. Add the macaroni and cook according to the package directions, just until al dente. Drain the pasta and set aside.

Meanwhile, place the cottage cheese in a small food processor or smoothie blender and blitz until smooth.

In a large saucepan over medium heat, melt the butter. Add the garlic and cook for 30 seconds. In a small bowl or glass measuring cup, whisk the milk, cornstarch, mustard powder, turmeric, and onion powder together, then pour into the pan. Bring to a simmer and cook, stirring occasionally, until slightly thickened, 3 to 5 minutes.

Turn the heat down to low and whisk in the cheddar cheese followed by the cottage cheese. Season with salt to taste, then add the cooked macaroni and stir well to combine.

In my professional experience, there are two things that can be found on every single person's list of favorite comfort foods: cheesy garlic bread and mac and cheese. Bringing them together in this book is a no-brainer.

Cheesy Garlic Bread Mac & Cheese

SERVES 4

FOR THE MAC

Kosher salt

10½ oz short pasta, such as medium shells

2 tablespoons butter

4 garlic cloves, divided

2 tablespoons all-purpose flour

2 cups milk, warmed

Freshly ground black pepper

1 teaspoon Dijon mustard

1 cup grated orange cheddar, preferably medium

½ cup grated Parmigiano-Reggiano

½ cup grated marble cheese

2 tablespoons finely chopped fresh parsley

FOR THE TOPPING

1 egg

2 tablespoons milk

Kosher salt

Freshly ground black pepper

2 tablespoons butter, room temperature

1 garlic clove, minced

2 teaspoons finely chopped fresh parsley, plus more for serving

3 slices Italian bread (see note)

½–1 cup grated marble cheese

Preheat your oven to 425°F and lightly grease a 2- to 3-quart casserole dish with nonstick cooking spray or softened butter.

For the mac, bring a large pot of salted water to a boil, then add the pasta and cook for 1 minute less than the package directions, or until the pasta is just slightly under al dente. Drain the pasta and set aside.

Meanwhile, in a large saucepan over medium heat, melt the butter. Grate in three cloves of garlic and cook for 30 seconds, then sprinkle in the flour and whisk to combine. Toast for 1 minute, then while continuing to whisk, slowly pour in the warm milk. Season with salt and pepper and bring to a light boil. Cook, whisking often, until thick, 4 to 5 minutes.

Once thickened, turn the heat down to low and whisk in the mustard and cheeses.

Grate in the remaining clove of garlic. Set your whisk aside and, using a heatproof spatula or a wooden spoon, stir in the parsley and pasta. Transfer to the prepared casserole dish and set aside.

For the topping, in a medium bowl, whisk the egg and milk together. Season with salt and pepper and set aside. In a small bowl, combine the butter, garlic, and parsley and spread onto the bread. Cut the bread into small cubes and add to the egg mixture, tossing to coat.

Top the casserole with the bread mixture, scatter with the grated marble cheese, and bake for 20 to 25 minutes, or until golden brown and bubbly. Allow the mac and cheese to rest for a few minutes before serving with extra parsley scattered overtop.

Note: If you have any store-bought garlic bread on hand, you can make the topping using a few slices of that.

Just because mac and cheese is the ultimate put-it-in-a-bowl-and-eat-it-on-the-couch food doesn't mean it can't have a bit of a snazz-up. Just bust out your hard pants and mix in the flavors of a caprese salad to make a mac worthy of the fanciest guests.

Caprese Mac & Cheese

SERVES 4

FOR THE MAC

Kosher salt

10½ oz short, ridged pasta, such as rotini or radiatori

2 tablespoons olive oil

2 garlic cloves, minced

2 tablespoons all-purpose flour

2 cups milk, warmed

Freshly ground black pepper

1 teaspoon Dijon mustard

1½ cups grated mozzarella

1 cup grated Parmigiano-Reggiano

3–4 tablespoons prepared pesto

1 cup cherry tomatoes, halved

FOR THE TOPPING

1 egg

2 tablespoons milk

Kosher salt

Freshly ground black pepper

2–3 slices Italian bread or focaccia, roughly torn into small pieces

½ teaspoon dried Italian seasoning

4½ oz bocconcini or fresh mozzarella, torn

½ cup cherry tomatoes, halved

Fresh basil or prepared pesto, for serving

Preheat your oven to 425°F and lightly grease a 2- to 3-quart casserole dish with nonstick cooking spray.

For the mac, bring a large pot of salted water to a boil, then add the pasta and cook for 1 minute less than the package directions, or until the pasta is just slightly under al dente. Drain the pasta and set aside.

Meanwhile, in a large saucepan over medium heat, heat the oil. Stir in the garlic and cook for 30 seconds, then sprinkle in the flour and whisk to combine. Toast for 1 minute, then while continuing to whisk, slowly pour in the warm milk. Season with salt and pepper and bring to a light boil. Cook, whisking often, until thick, 4 to 5 minutes.

Once thickened, turn the heat down to low and whisk in the mustard, mozzarella, and Parmigiano-Reggiano. Switch to a heatproof spatula or a wooden spoon and stir in the pesto, tomatoes, and cooked pasta. Transfer to the prepared casserole dish and set aside.

For the topping, in a medium bowl, whisk the egg and milk together. Season with salt and pepper and stir in the torn bread and Italian seasoning.

Top the mac and cheese with the bread mixture, scatter or nestle in the fresh mozzarella and tomatoes, and bake for 20 to 25 minutes, or until golden brown and bubbly. Allow the mac and cheese to rest for a few minutes before serving with fresh basil or extra pesto.

Who doesn't love a good charcuterie board? They are the easiest thing to throw together for snacky dinners or caszh hangouts, and they keep your friends busy while you frantically finish dinner prep. The only thing I don't love about them is all those random bits of cheese left on the board at the end of the night. The glory of this particular mac is that it's specifically designed to use up all those leftovers, giving them a second chance at life rather than being condemned to languish in the back of your cheese drawer for who knows how long.

Charcuterie Board Mac & Cheese

SERVES 4

FOR THE MAC

- Kosher salt
- 10½ oz short tube pasta, such as rigatoni, penne, or cavatappi
- 2 tablespoons butter
- 2 garlic cloves, minced
- 2 tablespoons all-purpose flour
- 2 cups milk, warmed
- Freshly ground black pepper
- Pinch freshly grated nutmeg
- 1 tablespoon grainy Dijon mustard
- 2–2½ cups grated or crumbled cheese, whatever combination you have
- 2½–3½ oz thinly sliced salami or prosciutto, diced
- ½ cup diced cornichons, green olives, or pickled onions

FOR THE TOPPING

- 1 egg
- 2 tablespoons whole milk
- Kosher salt
- Freshly ground black pepper
- 5–6 slices baguette, roughly torn into small pieces
- ½ cup grated cheese

Preheat your oven to 425°F and lightly grease a 2- to 3-quart casserole dish with nonstick cooking spray.

For the mac, bring a large pot of salted water to a boil, then add the pasta and cook for 1 minute less than the package directions, or until the pasta is just slightly under al dente. Drain the pasta and set aside.

Meanwhile, in a large saucepan over medium heat, melt the butter. Stir in the garlic and cook for 30 seconds, then sprinkle in the flour and whisk to combine. Toast for 1 minute, then while continuing to whisk, slowly pour in the warm milk. Season with salt, pepper, and nutmeg and bring to a light boil. Cook, whisking often, until thick, 4 to 5 minutes.

Once thickened, turn the heat down to low and whisk in the mustard and whatever blend of cheese you're using. Switch to a heatproof spatula or a wooden spoon and stir in the pasta, salami or prosciutto, and cornichons, olives, or pickled onions. Transfer to the prepared casserole dish and set aside.

For the topping, in a medium bowl, whisk the egg and milk together. Season with salt and pepper, then stir in the torn baguette and grated cheese.

Top the mac with the bread mixture and bake for 20 to 25 minutes, or until golden brown and bubbly. Allow the mac and cheese to rest for a few minutes before serving.

Note: The glory of this mac and cheese is that it will be a little different every time you make it, depending on whatever cheese you have left over. Any mixture of cheese will work, but try to have at least one variety that's on the stronger side to amp up the flavor.

Slightly Grown-Up Stovetop Mac
Cheesy Garlic Bread Mac & Cheese
A Southern Spin on Myra's Mac

Caprese Mac & Cheese
Charcuterie Board Mac & Cheese

Myra's mac and cheese is a perennial fave, and while the original is completely perfect as is, after 30+ years I thought it was about time for a little switch-up. Given the Ritz topping, the natural addition to this baked Berg classic is the flavor of that Southern staple, pimento cheese.

A Southern Spin on Myra's Mac

SERVES 4

- Kosher salt
- 1½ cups elbow macaroni
- 3 eggs
- 1½ cups milk
- ½ teaspoon mustard powder or 1½ teaspoons Dijon mustard
- ½ teaspoon garlic powder
- ½ teaspoon onion powder
- ¼ teaspoon cayenne pepper
- Freshly ground black pepper
- 3 cups grated orange cheddar, divided
- ¼ cup finely chopped roasted red peppers
- 1 jalapeño, finely chopped
- 20–25 Ritz crackers
- ¼ cup ground Parmesan (see note)
- ¼–½ teaspoon crushed red pepper flakes
- 6 tablespoons butter, melted
- Pinch smoked paprika

Preheat your oven to 400°F and grease a 9-inch square baking pan or 2-quart casserole dish with nonstick cooking spray.

Set a pot of water to boil over high heat, season well with salt, and cook the macaroni for about 1 minute less than the package directions indicate or just until a little under al dente, then drain and allow to cool slightly.

Meanwhile, in a bowl, whisk together the eggs, milk, mustard powder or Dijon, garlic powder, onion powder, and cayenne pepper. Season with salt and pepper.

When the pasta has cooled slightly, transfer it to the prepared baking pan. Scatter with 2 cups of the cheddar, the roasted red peppers, and the jalapeños and gently mix to evenly distribute. Pour the milk and egg mixture over the pasta and set aside while you prepare the topping.

For the topping, place the crackers in a bowl or a large zip-top bag and crush them up a bit. Add the ground Parmesan, red pepper flakes, and butter and mix well to combine. Finally, add the remaining cup of grated cheddar and mix to combine. Scatter the topping over the macaroni, add a pinch of smoked paprika, and bake for 35 to 40 minutes, or until set in the middle and golden brown on top.

Set aside to rest for a few minutes before serving.

Note: Unlike other baked mac and cheese recipes, my mom's is more of a cheesy, custardy, sliceable casserole than a saucy, spoonable number.

And Another Note! Whenever one of my recipes calls for ground Parmesan rather than Parmigiano-Reggiano, just know that I mean that shaky little container of Parm you find in the aisles of your local grocery store. I unabashedly love the stuff, but I know that a lot of people don't, so feel free to replace it with the real thing. Just make sure you use ground, not grated, cheese, as ground holds up better to the heat of the oven.

I never thought I'd describe a shade of green as thrilling, but here we are! A quick blanch in some boiling water and a trip through the blender turns earthy Tuscan kale into the brightest, most verdant green sauce you'll ever see. Seasoned with one of my favorite store-bought shortcuts, this dish is both fast and fancy.

Greens & Cheese Pasta

SERVES 4

FOR THE STRACCIATELLA

3½–4½ oz ball fresh mozzarella

Kosher salt

¼–½ cup whipping cream

FOR THE PASTA

1 bunch Tuscan kale

Kosher salt

12 oz rotini or other twisty pasta

4–6 tablespoons prepared pesto

½ cup finely grated Parmigiano-Reggiano, plus more for serving

Olive oil, for serving

Fresh basil, for serving

For the stracciatella, finely pull and shred the ball of fresh mozzarella and transfer to a bowl. Season with salt and pour enough cream overtop to generously coat the mozzarella. Stir to combine, then cover and refrigerate overnight. The stracciatella will keep for up to 3 days.

For the pasta, bring a large pot of water to a boil over high heat. Prepare the kale by removing the ribs and roughly chopping the leaves. Season the water well with salt and add the kale leaves. Cook for 30 seconds to 1 minute, until the kale is bright green and wilted. Remove the kale from the water and transfer to your blender.

Add the rotini to the boiling water and cook according to the package directions, or until al dente. Reserve about 1½ cups of the cooking liquid before draining the pasta. Return the pasta to the pot and set aside.

Add about ½ cup of the pasta cooking liquid to the blender along with the pesto, to taste, and blitz until very smooth, adding a few more splashes of the pasta cooking liquid as needed to reach a saucy consistency.

Add the sauce to the pasta along with the Parmigiano-Reggiano and toss well to combine. Serve topped with the stracciatella, a drizzle of olive oil, some more Parmigiano-Reggiano, and fresh basil.

Note: Stracciatella can be many things, from a gelato flavor to a comforting soup, but in this instance, it's that creamy dreamy filling bursting from a ball of burrata. While you can usually find it at specialty cheese shops, making it is a total breeze and way more affordable. Just be sure to prep it the day before so that the mozzarella can absorb some of the cream.

This recipe goes out to my mom, Myra Berg, who one time bought about five jars of roasted red peppers to make a recipe that she promptly lost. Rather than have those jars languish in the cupboard for years to come, I whipped up this romesco-esque sauce and took a cue from that viral baked feta recipe to really make a meal out of it.

Roasted Red Pepper Feta Pasta

SERVES 4

- ¼ cup roughly chopped almonds
- 1½ cups (about 12 fl oz) jarred roasted red peppers, drained
- ¼ cup roughly chopped oil-packed sundried tomatoes
- 2 garlic cloves, roughly chopped
- 1 small handful fresh flat-leaf parsley, roughly chopped, plus more for serving
- 1 lemon, zested and juiced
- ½ teaspoon smoked paprika
- Olive oil
- Kosher salt
- Freshly ground black pepper
- 7 oz block feta
- 12 oz long pasta, such as spaghetti or linguine

In a small pan over medium heat, toast the almonds until lightly browned and nutty smelling, 1 to 2 minutes. Set aside.

In the bowl of your food processor or in your high-speed blender, combine the roasted red peppers, sundried tomatoes, garlic, parsley, lemon zest, lemon juice, and smoked paprika. Pulse a few times to chop and mix. Add 3 tablespoons of oil and blend into a smooth sauce. Season to taste with salt and pepper, then transfer the sauce to a large baking pan or casserole dish. Nestle the feta in the center, drizzle with 1 tablespoon of oil, and set aside.

Bring a large pot of water to a boil over high heat and season well with salt. Add the pasta and cook according to the package directions, or until al dente. Reserve about 1 cup of the cooking liquid before draining the pasta.

Meanwhile, transfer the sauce and feta to the oven and broil on high for at least 5 minutes, or until the pasta is ready.

When the pasta is cooked and the feta is golden, transfer the pasta to the pan containing the sauce and add a splash of cooking liquid. Stir well to break up the feta and evenly combine, adding more pasta cooking liquid if needed to reach a saucy consistency.

Serve scattered with more parsley, if desired.

For as long as I can remember, breakfast for dinner has been a classic in our house. But while early morning staples like pancakes, French toast, and bacon and eggs typically take up the mantle, I think carbonara also counts. At its core, it's basically the bacon and eggs of the pasta world, so while it obviously makes a great breakfast for dinner, why not live life on a very low edge and try it as dinner for breakfast?

Shorty Carbonara

SERVES 4

- 5 oz guanciale or pancetta, diced (see note)
- Kosher salt
- 12 oz short pasta, such as mezzi rigatoni, medium shells, or penne
- 4 egg yolks
- ½ cup finely grated pecorino Romano
- ¼ cup finely grated Parmigiano-Reggiano, plus extra for serving
- 2 tablespoons finely chopped fresh parsley
- Freshly ground black pepper

Place a large pot of water over high heat and bring to a boil.

Add the guanciale or pancetta to a large sauté pan and turn the heat to medium-high. Cook until crisp, 5 to 6 minutes, then remove the pan from the heat and set aside.

Season the boiling water with salt and cook the pasta according to the package directions until al dente, reserving the pasta cooking liquid.

Meanwhile, in a large bowl, whisk together the egg yolks, pecorino, Parmigiano, and parsley, and season with salt and lots of pepper. Whisk in about ¼ cup of the hot pasta cooking liquid.

Place the pan with the meat back over medium-high heat and add the pasta. Toss to combine and coat the noodles with the hot fat. Pour the hot pasta mixture into the bowl with the egg mixture and quickly toss well to combine. Continue to toss until the sauce is creamy, adding more pasta cooking liquid as needed. If the sauce is not thickening up, you can transfer the pasta and sauce to the still-warm pan and toss. The residual heat of the pan should firm up the sauce a bit, but be careful not to scramble the eggs.

Serve immediately topped with more Parmigiano and black pepper.

Note: When cooking fattier meats like guanciale, pancetta, or bacon, start them in a cold pan. Slowly bringing the meat up to temperature lets the fat gently render out while the meat crisps up.

My ultimate comfort food as a kid was cheese tortellini doused in butter and loaded with shaky cheese. It was always the first thing I asked for when I was on the mend from whatever ailed me. While I've been known to make cheese tortellini from scratch, who really has that kind of time? When I'm in need of the comfort that only a plate of stuffed pasta can provide, I whip up some crespelle. Italy's answer to France's crepes, they are the easiest, most perfect vehicle for any cheesy or creamy stuffed pasta filling.

Ricotta Crespelle with Lemon Cream

SERVES 4

FOR THE CRESPELLE

2 eggs
1 cup milk
1 cup all-purpose flour
½ teaspoon kosher salt
1 tablespoon butter, melted
Butter or oil, for cooking

FOR THE FILLING

2 cups ricotta
1 cup finely grated Parmigiano-Reggiano
1 egg
2 garlic cloves, minced
½ lemon, zested and juiced
3 tablespoons finely chopped fresh basil
2 tablespoons finely chopped fresh parsley
Pinch freshly grated nutmeg
Kosher salt
Freshly ground black pepper

For the crespelle, in a bowl, whisk the eggs and milk together. Add the flour and salt and whisk well until smooth, then stir in the melted butter. Set the batter aside at room temperature for 1 hour or in the fridge for up to 2 days.

To cook the crespelle, place a medium nonstick skillet over medium heat. Very lightly grease the pan with butter or oil and pour a generous ¼ cup of batter into the pan. Quickly tilt and swirl the pan to evenly coat it with the batter. Cook for about 1 minute on the first side, or until lightly golden brown, then flip and continue to cook for 30 seconds on the second side. Transfer the crespelle to a plate and continue cooking the remaining batter. You should end up with eight or nine crespelle.

Preheat your oven to 375°F.

For the filling, in a medium bowl, combine the ricotta, Parmigiano-Reggiano, egg, and garlic. Add the lemon zest and juice, then stir in the basil and parsley and season with nutmeg, salt, and pepper.

Divide the filling evenly among the crespelle and spread into an even layer. Fold the crespelle in half and then in half again to form triangles, and place them in a slightly overlapping row on a sheet pan. Bake for 15 to 20 minutes, just until heated through and lightly crisp around the edges.

CONTINUED

FOR THE SAUCE & SERVING

1 cup cream, 10% or higher

1 lemon

1 garlic clove

1 cup finely grated Parmigiano-Reggiano, plus more for serving

Pinch freshly grated nutmeg

Kosher salt

Freshly ground black pepper

Fresh basil, for serving

Meanwhile, prepare the sauce. Place the cream in a small saucepan. Using a vegetable peeler, remove the zest from the lemon in long strips and add to the cream. Add the garlic, leaving the clove whole for a milder garlic flavor or smashing or roughly chopping it first for a stronger garlic flavor. Place the saucepan over medium heat and bring to a simmer. Simmer for 10 to 15 minutes, or until the cream has reduced slightly and thickened. If the cream reduces too much at any point, just add another splash of cream.

When the crespelle are done, use a slotted spoon to remove the lemon zest and garlic clove from the cream. Whisk in the cheese and season with nutmeg, salt, and pepper.

Divide the sauce over four serving plates. Top with two crespelle per plate and scatter with basil, lemon zest, and more cheese, if desired.

Note: There are tons of ways to get ahead with this dish. You can make the batter up to 2 days ahead of cooking, and cook the crespelle up to 3 days ahead if stored in the fridge or up to 1 month ahead if stored in the freezer. Even the stuffed crespelle can be made 1 day in advance and simply heated in the oven before serving.

Gnocchi is a true gift to indecisive starch lovers like me who have a hard time choosing between their favorite comforting carbs. Pasta or potatoes? Why not both?!

Spicy Gnocchi alla Vodka

SERVES 4

FOR THE GNOCCHI

4 medium (about 8 oz each) baking potatoes

2 egg yolks

1 cup all-purpose flour, plus more if needed

1 teaspoon kosher salt

¼ teaspoon freshly ground black pepper

Pinch freshly grated nutmeg

FOR THE PANGRATTATO

2 tablespoons butter

½ cup panko breadcrumbs

½ cup finely grated Parmigiano-Reggiano

½ lemon, zested

2 tablespoons finely chopped fresh basil

For the gnocchi, preheat your oven to 425°F. Place the potatoes on a rimmed sheet pan and pierce them a few times with a fork. Bake for 45 minutes to 1 hour, until fork tender, flipping halfway through.

Cut the potatoes in half, set aside for a few minutes until cool enough to handle, then scoop the potato flesh from the skins. Using a potato ricer or masher, rice or thoroughly mash the potatoes until smooth. Transfer the potatoes to a large bowl and allow them to cool fully to room temperature.

In a small bowl, lightly beat the egg yolks, then drizzle them over the potatoes and lightly mix. Sprinkle 1 cup of the flour overtop and season with the salt, pepper, and nutmeg. Mix just until a soft but not too sticky dough comes together, adding more flour if needed. Do not overwork the dough, as that will lead to dense gnocchi.

Lightly dust a rimmed sheet pan with flour and divide the dough into four pieces. On a lightly floured work surface, roll each piece into a ¾-inch-thick log. Cut each log into roughly ¾-inch pieces and transfer them to the prepared sheet pan. Set aside.

For the pangrattato, in a small pan over medium-high heat, melt the butter. Add the panko and toast, stirring often, until golden brown, about 1 minute. Transfer to a dish to cool, then stir in the Parmigiano-Reggiano, lemon zest, and basil.

CONTINUED

FOR THE SAUCE

2 tablespoons butter

1 large shallot, finely minced

Kosher salt

Freshly ground black pepper

3 garlic cloves, finely minced

1 can (5 fl oz) tomato paste

1–2 teaspoons crushed red pepper flakes or 1–3 tablespoons chili peppers in oil

¼ cup vodka

½ cup whipping cream

½ cup finely grated Parmigiano-Reggiano

2 tablespoons finely chopped fresh basil

For the sauce, in a large high-sided pan over medium heat, melt the butter. Add the shallots, season with salt and pepper, and cook until lightly golden brown, 2 to 3 minutes. Stir in the garlic and cook for 30 seconds, then stir in the tomato paste and red pepper flakes or chilies. Cook for about 2 minutes to intensify the tomato flavor, then carefully deglaze the pan with the vodka. Cook for 1 to 2 minutes to let the alcohol cook off, then turn the heat down to low and stir in the whipping cream. Keep the sauce warm over low heat while you cook the gnocchi.

Set a large pot of water to boil over high heat and season well with salt. Cook the gnocchi for 3 to 4 minutes, or for about 1 minute after they have floated to the surface. Using a slotted spoon, transfer the cooked gnocchi directly to the sauce along with about ¼ cup of the gnocchi cooking liquid (using a ladle). Finish with the Parmigiano-Reggiano, basil, and a final seasoning of salt and pepper. If the sauce is a little thick, stir in a few splashes of the cooking liquid.

Serve immediately scattered with the pangrattato.

Note: For quicker baked potatoes, you can use your microwave. Pierce the potatoes a few times with a fork and microwave on high for 8 minutes, or until fork tender, flipping halfway through. For an even quicker dish as a whole, feel free to pick up a pack of premade gnocchi from the grocery store.

While homemade gnocchi is relatively simple to make, this recipe can easily become a weeknight favorite by swapping homemade gnocchi for store-bought.

The Atlantic Codfather
says his family's success
depends on schools

Gone Fishin'

Some of my favorite childhood memories include a fishing pole slung over my shoulder with a tackle box in tow. Nowadays, I leave the catch of the day to the pros and stick to the stove for flavor-packed fish in a flash.

Sheet Pan Salmon Niçoise-ish 165
Caesar Salad Salmon 161
Roasted Salmon with Green Olive Gremolata 164

Roasted Salmon 4 Ways

Chicken used to be the jeans and T-shirt of home cooking. It was a staple that everyone had their own version of, but just like with fashion, tastes evolve and salmon has taken over the table.

Note: If you're looking to feed a crowd, double up any of the recipes and roast a larger piece or whole side of salmon for 15 to 18 minutes, then broil on high for 1 to 2 minutes, or until golden and cooked to your liking.

Deciding what counts as breakfast for dinner is all in the eye of the beholder. You can be a purist or, like me, be more of a vibes gal. For those days when I want to feel like an adult but still indulge in breakfast-y eats, this schmear-inspired salmon hits the spot.

Bagel Shop Salmon

SERVES 4

FOR THE SALMON

Four 7 oz salmon fillets
Kosher salt
Freshly ground black pepper
1 tablespoon butter, melted
1 tablespoon toasted sesame oil
4 tablespoons sesame seeds
2–3 tablespoons capers

FOR SERVING

1 small red onion, thinly sliced
½ cucumber, thinly sliced
Kosher salt
Freshly ground black pepper
1 lemon
1 cup plain Greek yogurt or skyr
1 tablespoon prepared horseradish
1 garlic clove, minced
Fresh dill

For the salmon, preheat your oven to 400°F and lightly grease a sheet pan or line it with parchment paper.

Dry off the salmon fillets using paper towel, then arrange them on the sheet pan, skin side down, and season with salt and pepper. In a small bowl, whisk together the melted butter and toasted sesame oil, then spoon this over the salmon fillets. Set the bowl off to the side. Scatter the salmon with the sesame seeds and set aside.

Dry the capers well with some paper towel and transfer to the bowl containing any remaining butter and sesame oil. Toss well to evenly coat the capers, then scatter them onto the sheet pan. Roast the salmon and capers for 12 to 15 minutes, or until the salmon is cooked through to your liking and the capers are lightly crisp.

Meanwhile, prepare the veg and sauce for serving. Place the onions and cucumbers in a nonreactive bowl (i.e., either glass or plastic) and season with salt and pepper. Using a vegetable peeler, remove the zest from about half of the lemon and thinly slice the zest into strips. (You can also use a rasp to zest the lemon, but I'm partial to the bigger pieces of lemon peel. They somehow taste fresher and are less punchy than finer zest.) Add the lemon zest to the bowl along with the juice from the lemon half, toss and scrunch the veg in it to evenly coat, and set aside to lightly pickle while the salmon roasts and you prepare the sauce.

For the sauce, place the yogurt or skyr in a bowl along with the horseradish, garlic, and the juice from the remaining lemon half. Season with salt and pepper and stir well to combine.

Serve the salmon and crispy capers scattered with dill, with the pickled salad and sauce on the side.

Note: Whenever you're pickling or mixing something highly acidic, you'll want to use a nonreactive bowl. Glass, plastic, or ceramic will do—you just want to avoid metal bowls, as they can react with the acid in the recipe and lead to a metallic taste.

When you think of a big bowl of something comforting, I realize that the first thing that comes to mind isn't necessarily a salad, but as you see throughout this book, I truly think salads can be the star of your next couch dinner. And if I'm celebrating the world of indulgent salads, Caesar is obviously going to make a few appearances. The creamy, funky, peppery dressing already includes the wrong-but-oh-so-right pairing of fish and cheese, so why not double down and Caesar up some salmon too!

Caesar Salad Salmon

SERVES 4

FOR THE SALMON

1 tablespoon olive oil

½ cup panko breadcrumbs

¾ teaspoon garlic powder, divided

Kosher salt

Freshly ground black pepper

¼ cup mayonnaise

¼ cup finely grated Parmigiano-Reggiano

1 anchovy fillet, minced

1 lemon, zested

Four 7 oz salmon fillets

FOR THE SALAD

2 anchovy fillets, minced

1 garlic clove, minced

½–1 lemon, juiced

1 tablespoon red wine vinegar

1 teaspoon Dijon mustard

3 tablespoons mayonnaise

2 tablespoons olive oil

¼ cup finely grated Parmigiano-Reggiano, plus more for serving

Kosher salt

Freshly ground black pepper

1 head or 2 hearts romaine lettuce, roughly chopped

For the salmon, preheat your oven to 400°F.

Place a small skillet over medium-high heat. Add the oil, panko, and ¼ teaspoon of garlic powder, season with salt and pepper, and toast for 2 to 3 minutes, or until golden, stirring often. Transfer the panko to a small bowl and set aside.

Meanwhile, in a medium bowl, whisk together the mayonnaise, Parmigiano, anchovy, lemon zest, and remaining ½ teaspoon of garlic powder. Season with salt and lots of black pepper.

Lightly oil a sheet pan and add on the salmon fillets, skin side down. Alternatively, or if you are using skinless salmon, line the sheet pan with parchment paper. Evenly spread the mayonnaise mixture over the salmon and scatter with the panko. Roast for 12 to 15 minutes, until cooked to your liking.

While the salmon cooks, prepare the salad. In a large bowl, whisk together the anchovies, garlic, juice of half a lemon, and red wine vinegar. Whisk in the Dijon, mayonnaise, oil, and Parmigiano, and season to taste with salt and lots of pepper. Add the lettuce and set aside.

When ready to serve, toss the salad, adding more lemon juice and cheese, if desired. Transfer the salad to serving plates, top with additional Parmigiano-Reggiano and pepper, and serve alongside the salmon.

Roasted Salmon with Green Olive Gremolata
Sheet Pan Salmon Niçoise-ish

Bagel Shop Salmon
Caesar Salad Salmon

If you've never had gremolata, it's basically an herby, savory Italian sprinkle often reserved for low-and-slow braised dishes like osso buco. With bright and briny green olives and a glug of peppery extra virgin olive oil added to the mix, this classic condiment gets a bit of a refresh, making it the perfect pairing for an equally classic roasted salmon.

Roasted Salmon with Green Olive Gremolata

SERVES 4

FOR THE GREMOLATA

1 large handful fresh parsley
1 cup pitted green olives
2 garlic cloves, minced
1 lemon, zested
4–6 tablespoons olive oil
Kosher salt
Freshly ground black pepper

FOR THE SALMON

1 lemon, juiced
2 garlic cloves, minced
½ teaspoon crushed red pepper flakes
2 tablespoons olive oil
Kosher salt
Freshly ground black pepper
Four 7 oz salmon fillets

Preheat your oven to 400°F and lightly oil a sheet pan.

For the gremolata, finely chop together the parsley, olives, garlic, and lemon zest. Transfer to a bowl and stir in enough oil to reach a saucy consistency. Season with salt and pepper and set aside in the fridge while you prepare the salmon.

For the salmon, in a large bowl, whisk together the lemon juice, garlic, red pepper flakes, and oil, and season with salt and pepper. Add the salmon fillets and toss well to evenly coat in the lemon mixture. Transfer the salmon to the prepared sheet pan, skin side down.

Roast the salmon for 12 to 15 minutes, or until cooked to your liking.

Serve the salmon hot or chilled, with the gremolata spooned overtop.

Note: If the punchy flavor of raw garlic is too much for you, add a squidge of lemon juice to the gremolata to balance it out.

I feel like anytime someone new is coming over for dinner, three things happen in very quick succession in my mind. First, I am convinced I've forgotten how to cook. Second, I frantically hide my stacks of papers and books and that pile of clean clothes that I keep on The Clean Clothes Chair™ (iykyk). And finally, I remember that France exists and knows a thing or two about flavors. So if you ever want to seem fancy and like your closet floor is *not* currently occupied by your poorly hidden shame piles, may I suggest this easy roasted spin on the flavors of salade niçoise.

Sheet Pan Salmon Niçoise-ish

SERVES 4

FOR THE SALMON

Four 7 oz salmon fillets
½ cup dry white wine
½ lemon, zested
3 garlic cloves, smashed and roughly chopped
1 teaspoon herbes de Provence
¼ cup olive oil
Kosher salt
Freshly ground black pepper

FOR THE VEG & BASIL PISTOU

1½ lb mini potatoes
½ teaspoon herbes de Provence
1 sprig fresh rosemary
6–7 tablespoons olive oil, divided
2 shallots
2 handfuls green beans, trimmed
1 cup cherry tomatoes, halved
3 tablespoons capers
Kosher salt
Freshly ground black pepper
1 cup loosely packed fresh basil
1 lemon, zested
1 garlic clove, minced
½ cup niçoise or kalamata olives

For the salmon, place the fillets in a shallow dish or large zip-top bag along with the wine, lemon zest, garlic, herbes de Provence, and ¼ cup of oil. Season with salt and pepper and flip or gently massage to combine and evenly coat the fish in the marinade. Set aside in the fridge for at least 15 minutes or up to 2 hours.

Meanwhile, place a large sheet pan in your oven and preheat it to 400°F.

For the veg, halve the potatoes and place them in a large bowl along with the herbes de Provence and rosemary. Drizzle with 2 tablespoons of olive oil, season with salt and pepper, and toss well to combine. Carefully remove the hot sheet pan from the oven and transfer the potatoes to the pan, setting the bowl to the side. Roast the potatoes for 25 minutes, or until a little tender and golden brown.

While the potatoes roast, cut each shallot into eight wedges and add them to the bowl along with the green beans, cherry tomatoes, and capers. Drizzle with 1 tablespoon of oil, season with salt and pepper, and toss to combine. Remove the salmon from the marinade and pat dry with paper towel.

After the potatoes have roasted for 25 minutes, remove the sheet pan from the oven and give the potatoes a toss. Add the green beans, tomatoes, and capers and nestle in the salmon fillets, skin side down. Return the pan to the oven for 12 to 15 minutes, or until the salmon and veg are cooked to your liking.

While the salmon roasts, make the basil pistou. Place the basil, lemon zest, and garlic in a small food processor and blitz to chop. Drizzle in the remaining 3 to 4 tablespoons of oil and blitz to a slightly chunky, saucy consistency. Season with salt and pepper and set aside.

To serve, arrange the roasted veg and salmon on plates and scatter with the olives. Drizzle or dot with the basil pistou and a squidge of lemon juice, if desired.

Comfort and convenience go together like, well, fish and chips. While that sometimes means walking up the street to one of the three chip shops within a four-block radius of my house, I always like having some things stashed in the freezer and pantry so that I can throw together a quick dinner whenever a craving strikes.

Get-Ahead Fish & Chips

SERVES 4 (WITH LEFTOVER FISH)

FOR THE FISH

3 lb cod or haddock
¼ cup butter
4 cups panko breadcrumbs
2 teaspoons garlic powder
Kosher salt
Freshly ground black pepper
3 eggs
¾ cup mayonnaise
2 tablespoons Dijon mustard

FOR THE FISH & CHIPS

1½ lb fingerling or baby potatoes, halved
Kosher salt
2 tablespoons olive oil
½ cup mayonnaise
½ lemon, zested and juiced
3 tablespoons chopped dill pickles
2 tablespoons capers, chopped
2 tablespoons finely chopped fresh parsley
2 tablespoons finely chopped fresh dill
Freshly ground black pepper

Line a sheet pan with parchment paper and set aside.

For the fish, prepare the fish by cutting it into eight to ten relatively equal portions, then set aside in the fridge.

In a large skillet over medium heat, melt the butter. Add the panko and garlic powder, season with salt and pepper, and cook, stirring often, until the panko is golden brown, about 5 minutes. Transfer the panko to a shallow dish or square baking pan and allow to cool to room temperature.

Meanwhile, in a separate shallow dish, whisk together the eggs, mayonnaise, and Dijon and season with ½ teaspoon each of salt and pepper. Dry off each piece of fish, using paper towel. Dip the fish in the egg mixture, then press into the panko to coat and transfer to the prepared sheet pan.

If cooking the fish tonight, place in the fridge. If enjoying it later, cover the pan lightly with plastic wrap and place in the freezer. Once the cod is frozen, transfer to a heavy-duty freezer bag and store in the freezer for up to 3 months.

For the fish and chips, place a large sheet pan on the bottom rack of your oven and preheat it to 425°F.

Place the potatoes in a large saucepan and cover with cold tap water. Season well with salt and bring to a boil over high heat. Cook until the potatoes are fork tender, 10 to 15 minutes. Drain the potatoes and allow them to steam dry for 1 to 2 minutes, then transfer to a large bowl. Add the oil, season with salt, and toss well to coat.

Remove the hot pan from the oven and add the potatoes. Make space in the center, add the fish, then roast until cooked through—13 to 15 minutes for fresh, 18 to 22 minutes for frozen.

Prepare the tartar sauce in a small bowl by whisking the mayonnaise, lemon zest, lemon juice, pickles, capers, parsley, and dill. Season with salt, if needed, and pepper. Serve the crispy fish and potatoes hot from the oven with the tartar sauce on the side.

For a bit of green, boil up some classic frozen peas to serve alongside the fish and chips.

Fish pie is a UK classic. It's not seen much around these parts, but I think it's about time we change that. While the dish commits the supposed cardinal culinary sin of mixing fish with cheese, something so wrong never tasted so right.

Fish Pie

SERVES 4

FOR THE POTATOES

1½ lb yellow potatoes
2 garlic cloves, peeled
Kosher salt
2–3 tablespoons butter
¾ cup buttermilk or milk
¼ cup sour cream
1–2 tablespoons prepared horseradish, optional
1 cup grated extra-old white cheddar

FOR THE FILLING

2 tablespoons butter
1 yellow onion, finely diced
Kosher salt
Freshly ground black pepper
2 tablespoons all-purpose flour
2 cups milk
1 tablespoon Dijon mustard
7 oz skinless salmon
7 oz cod or haddock
3½ oz smoked haddock or hot-smoked salmon
1 cup frozen peas
3–4 tablespoons chopped fresh chives
2 tablespoons chopped fresh parsley
1 lemon, zested

Preheat your oven to 375°F and lightly grease a 3-quart casserole dish with nonstick cooking spray.

For the potatoes, peel and cut the potatoes into large, roughly equal chunks and place in a large pot. Add the garlic cloves, top with about 1 inch of cold tap water, season well with salt, and bring to a boil over high heat. Once boiling, turn the heat down to medium-high, top the pot with an off-kilter lid, and boil until the potatoes are tender and break apart easily when pierced with a fork. This should take 15 to 20 minutes, depending on your potatoes.

When tender, drain the potatoes and garlic, then transfer back to the pot. Add the butter and, using a hand masher, roughly mash the potatoes. Add the buttermilk or milk, sour cream, and horseradish, if using, and continue to mash until smooth. For a smoother mash, switch to a hand mixer and whip on medium just until the potatoes reach your desired consistency, being careful not to overwhip, as this will cause the potatoes to become gluey. Switch to a spoon or spatula and stir in the cheddar. Season to taste with salt. Set aside.

For the filling, in a medium saucepan over medium heat, melt the butter. Add the onions, season with salt and pepper, and cook down until softened and lightly translucent, 5 to 6 minutes. Stir in the flour and allow it to toast for 1 minute, then slowly whisk in the milk. Bring the mixture to a simmer and allow it to bubble away for 2 to 3 minutes, just until slightly thickened. Whisk in the Dijon, season well with salt and pepper, and set aside.

Meanwhile, dice the fresh salmon and cod or haddock into 1-inch chunks and roughly flake apart the smoked fish. Add the fish to the prepared casserole dish along with the peas, chives, parsley, and lemon zest. Pour the thickened milk mixture overtop and gently stir to combine.

Dollop or pipe the mashed potatoes over the filling and bake for 35 to 40 minutes, or until the top is lightly golden and the filling is bubbling. Allow the pie to rest for 5 minutes before serving, and garnish with extra chopped chives, if desired.

Note: Many fish pies have shrimp in them, so if that's your bag, swap out 3½ oz of the fresh fish for chopped raw shrimp.

Meaty Morsels

Let's get to the meat of the matter.

There's nothing like tucking into a pastry-topped stew rich with bacon, chicken, and whatever green veg you've got lying around. This recipe takes the classic to new heights by loading the puff pastry with crispy bacon and green onions, making every layer of this pie a total winner.

Chicken & Bacon Pot Pie

SERVES 6

- 1–2 sheets frozen puff pastry
- 6 slices bacon, diced
- 6–8 boneless, skinless chicken thighs
- Kosher salt
- Freshly ground black pepper
- 2 bunches green onions, divided
- 1 tablespoon butter
- 2 garlic cloves, minced
- Pinch freshly grated nutmeg
- 3 tablespoons all-purpose flour
- ½ cup dry white wine
- 2 cups chicken broth (page 45 or store-bought)
- 2–3 cups lightly packed dark, leafy greens
- 1 cup frozen peas
- ½ cup sour cream
- 1 tablespoon Dijon mustard
- 2 tablespoons finely chopped fresh parsley
- 1 egg
- 1 tablespoon water

Note: If you don't want to cook up chicken thighs, this recipe is a perfect use for the Poached Chicken & Broth on page 45. Or, to make things even easier, use a store-bought rotisserie chicken.

Thaw the puff pastry according to the package directions and store in the fridge until ready to use. For a thicker crust on the pot pie, thaw two sheets. For a thinner crust, thaw one sheet.

Preheat your oven to 400°F.

Add the bacon to a large sauté pan or braiser and place over medium heat. Cook until the bacon is crisp, then use a slotted spoon to remove it from the pan. Season the chicken thighs with salt and pepper and sear in the bacon fat until golden on both sides and cooked through, 4 to 5 minutes per side. Set the chicken aside with the bacon to rest.

Set two green onions aside and slice the rest on the diagonal. Add the butter to the pan along with the sliced green onions and garlic, and season with salt, pepper, and a pinch of nutmeg. Cook down until slightly softened, 1 to 2 minutes.

Stir in the flour and toast for 1 minute, then deglaze the pan with the wine. Allow the wine to cook down for 1 to 2 minutes, then add the broth and bring to a boil. Add the greens and peas and cook just to wilt down. Stir in the sour cream, Dijon, and parsley and turn the heat down to low.

Dice or shred the chicken and add it to the pan. Set a few tablespoons of the crispy bacon aside and add the rest to the pan.

Finely chop the remaining crispy bacon and green onions. Unroll the puff pastry. If using one sheet, scatter the bacon and green onions across half of it. Fold the other half on top and roll out the pastry so that it is roughly the same size as the original piece. If using two sheets, simply scatter the bacon and green onions over one sheet and place the second on top, pressing well to adhere.

In a small bowl, beat the egg and water together to make an egg wash. Drape the bacon and green onion–studded puff pastry over the pan, cut a small vent in the center, and quickly brush with the egg wash.

Bake the pot pie for 30 minutes, or until the pastry is golden brown. Allow the pot pie to rest for 5 to 10 minutes before serving.

The thing I love most about cooking is that there's always something new to discover. Whether it's a new flavor combination or cooking technique, I'm so lucky that I get to learn from the many chefs and cooks I've come to know over the years. For instance, I thought I knew how to cook a mean chicken thigh, but then my bud, the amazing recipe developer Sonia Wong, showed me a cold pan method that leads to the most shatteringly crisp chicken skin ever. Using this new method with a timeless flavor combination brings a fresh spin to a soup-can staple.

Chicken & Mushroom Casserole

SERVES 4 TO 6

6 bone-in, skin-on chicken thighs
Kosher salt
Freshly ground black pepper
1 yellow onion, diced
1 tablespoon butter
8 oz cremini mushrooms, sliced
1 tablespoon finely chopped fresh sage
2 garlic cloves, thinly sliced
2 tablespoons soy sauce
1 cup long-grain white rice
2 cups mushroom broth (see note)
½ cup milk
¼–½ teaspoon smoked paprika
2 tablespoons finely chopped fresh parsley

Preheat your oven to 375°F and set out a large cast-iron skillet.

Dry the chicken with a few pieces of paper towel and season with salt and pepper. Add the chicken to the dry, cold skillet, skin side down, and place over medium heat. Allow the chicken to cook, undisturbed, for about 10 minutes, or until the edges are golden. Remove the seared chicken from the pan and set aside, skin side up. The chicken will not be fully cooked, but don't worry—it will finish in the oven.

Add the onions to the pan, season with salt and pepper, and cook down until softened and lightly golden, about 5 minutes. Add the butter, mushrooms, and sage, turn the heat up to medium-high, and cook for 5 to 7 minutes, or until golden. Add the garlic and soy sauce and cook just until the soy sauce has reduced, about 30 seconds. Stir in the rice and lightly toast for 1 minute, then remove from the heat.

Pour the broth and milk into the pan and stir to combine. Place the chicken on top, seared side up, and cover the pan with a tight-fitting lid or aluminum foil. Transfer to the oven and cook, covered, for 40 minutes. Remove the lid and continue to cook for 10 minutes, or until the chicken is cooked through, the rice is tender, and the liquid has been absorbed.

Serve in the pan scattered with smoked paprika and parsley.

Note: Most grocery stores now carry mushroom broth, but if you can't find it, you have a couple of options. You can substitute it with chicken broth or, if you can find dried mushrooms, soak ½ oz of dried mushrooms in 2½ cups of hot water for 30 minutes. Squeeze out the reconstituted mushrooms, chop them up, and add them to the pan along with the fresh mushrooms. The remaining liquid is a rich mushroom broth that is perfect in this recipe.

There are a couple of dishes that we Bergs break out anytime someone needs a bit of comfort: one is my mom's classic mac and cheese, which I wrote about in my second cookbook, *Well Seasoned*; the other is any form of chicken Parmesan. If either of these are gracing my table, it's only a matter of time before you hear the slippered feet of my husband, Aaron, and my mom, Myra, come running. This recipe is a mash-up of those two classics. Myra's signature Ritz and cheddar topping for her mac and cheese gets repurposed as a crunchy chick-Parm-esque coating for chicken and keeps every belly in my house feeling cozy and content.

Cheddar Ritz Chicken

SERVES 4

- 4 boneless, skinless chicken breasts
- Kosher salt
- Freshly ground black pepper
- 2 eggs
- ¼ cup mayonnaise
- 1 tablespoon Dijon mustard
- 40 Ritz crackers
- 1 cup grated cheddar
- ½ cup ground Parmesan, a.k.a. shaky cheese (see note on page 7)
- ½ teaspoon garlic powder
- 8 tablespoons butter, melted

Preheat your oven to 425°F and grease a large sheet pan with nonstick cooking spray.

Butterfly the chicken breasts and pound to a scant ½ inch thick. Season the chicken with salt and pepper and set aside.

In a shallow dish or pie plate, beat the eggs, mayonnaise, and Dijon.

Crush the crackers to a fine crumb and transfer to a separate shallow dish or pie plate. Stir in the cheddar, Parmesan, and garlic powder, then pour in the butter and stir well to evenly combine.

Working with one piece at a time, dip the chicken in the egg mixture and then in the cracker coating, pressing well to adhere as much of the coating as possible. Transfer the coated chicken to the prepared sheet pan and continue with the remaining chicken pieces, leaving a few inches of space between each piece on the pan. Once all the chicken has been coated, scatter any remaining crumbs overtop.

Bake the chicken for 15 to 18 minutes, or until golden brown and crisp and the internal temperature of the chicken reaches 165°F. Allow the chicken to rest for 5 minutes before serving.

If you're like me, you've got to have a sauce. Whisk ½ cup of mayo with ¼ cup of Dijon mustard. Add about ½ teaspoon of smoked paprika and a bit of hot sauce and honey for some spicy sweetness.

There is only one rule when it comes to BBQ'd chicken: do not under any circumstances wear a white shirt. I mean, if you don't end up wearing some sauce, you're not doing it right.

Classic BBQ'd Chicken

SERVES 4

4 skin-on chicken leg quarters
Olive oil
1 tablespoon chili powder
1 tablespoon smoked paprika
½ teaspoon ground cumin
Kosher salt
Freshly ground black pepper
1 small yellow onion, finely diced
3 garlic cloves, finely minced
¼ cup light-flavored beer, such as a lager (see note)
1 cup ketchup
¼ cup apple cider vinegar
2 tablespoons dark brown sugar, packed
2 tablespoons molasses

Dry the chicken with a few pieces of paper towel and drizzle with about 1 tablespoon of olive oil. In a small bowl, combine the chili powder, smoked paprika, and cumin. Scatter about 2 teaspoons of this mixture onto the chicken, season with salt and pepper, and massage the seasoning into the chicken. Set aside for about 20 minutes to take off the chill of the fridge.

Heat your grill to medium. Lightly oil the grates and add the chicken, bone side down. Close the lid and cook for 30 minutes. Things might get smoky, but that's okay.

Meanwhile, in a medium saucepan over medium heat, heat 1 tablespoon of olive oil. Add the onions, season with salt and pepper, and cook until soft, about 5 minutes. Add the garlic and the remaining spice blend and cook for an additional 1 to 2 minutes to toast the spices. Carefully pour in the beer and scrape any bits off the bottom of the pan. Stir in the ketchup, vinegar, brown sugar, and molasses and bring the mixture to a boil. Turn the heat down to low, cover, and simmer for 20 minutes, stirring occasionally.

Divide the sauce into two separate bowls and set one aside. After the chicken has been grilling for 30 minutes, use one of the bowls of sauce to begin basting the chicken every 5 minutes or so, until the internal temperature of the chicken reaches 165°F. If the chicken or the sauce is browning too quickly, lower the heat.

Once cooked, remove the chicken to a cutting board and set aside to rest for 10 minutes before serving with the reserved sauce (discard any leftover basting sauce).

Note: If you don't keep beer on hand, swap it out with water and add a touch more vinegar and sugar to the mix.

Aaron's always been a real stew guy. In fact, when I asked him if that was an accurate statement, he proudly proclaimed, "Gimme that thick soup!" So it's no surprise that his favorite dish from the restaurant where we got married is their cassoulet. It's a rich stew-ish dish from the south of France, but it takes hours, if not days, to make. Since nobody has time for that, this recipe quickly delivers a pot of deliciousness in under an hour.

Quick Cassoulet

SERVES 4

- 2 slices bacon, diced
- 2 skin-on chicken leg quarters or 4 bone-in, skin-on chicken thighs
- Kosher salt
- Freshly ground black pepper
- 2–4 (3½ oz each) sausages
- 2 small yellow onions, diced
- 2 celery stalks, diced
- 1 carrot, diced
- 2–3 sprigs fresh thyme
- 2 garlic cloves, minced
- 1 tablespoon tomato paste
- 2 teaspoons smoked paprika
- Pinch freshly grated nutmeg
- ½ cup dry white wine
- 1½ cups chicken broth (page 45 or store-bought) , plus more if needed
- 1 can (14 fl oz) white kidney beans, drained and rinsed
- 3 tablespoons finely chopped fresh parsley, divided
- 2 thick slices crusty bread, plus more for serving

Note: If you don't have a braiser or Dutch oven, prepare the cassoulet in a large frying pan or saucepot, then transfer to a casserole dish to finish in the oven.

Preheat your oven to 350°F.

Place the bacon in a large braiser, cast-iron skillet, or Dutch oven and set over medium heat. Cook, stirring often, until the bacon is crisp, 5 to 6 minutes. Using a slotted spoon, remove the bacon from the pan and set aside.

If using chicken leg quarters, split the thighs from the drums. Season the chicken with salt and pepper and add to the pan, skin side down, along with the sausages. Sear until golden brown and a good amount of chicken fat has rendered out. This should take 7 to 8 minutes. At this point, the chicken and sausages will not be cooked through, but set them aside with the bacon. Carefully transfer 1 to 2 tablespoons of fat from the pan into a small bowl—you'll use it later.

Add the onions, celery, and carrots to the pan. Season with salt and pepper and add the thyme sprigs. Cook, stirring occasionally, until softened and lightly golden brown, 5 to 8 minutes. Add the garlic, tomato paste, paprika, and nutmeg, turn the heat up to medium-high, and toast for 1 minute, then deglaze the pan with the white wine. Allow the wine to reduce by half, then pour in the chicken broth.

Add the beans, 2 tablespoons of parsley, and the bacon and stir well to combine. If needed, add a little more chicken broth to cover. Nestle in the chicken and sausages, making sure the chicken is skin side up, and bring to a simmer.

Meanwhile, tear the bread into small chunks and toss with the remaining 1 tablespoon of parsley and 1 to 2 tablespoons of the reserved chicken fat. Season with salt and pepper and scatter the bread over the simmering beans and meat.

Transfer the pan to the oven and cook for 30 to 35 minutes, or until everything is golden brown and the chicken and sausages are cooked through and very tender.

Allow the cassoulet to rest for 10 minutes before serving with more crusty bread.

Salisbury Steak & Mushroom Meatballs 190

Spaghetti & Not Meatballs 192

Pork Souvlaki Meatballs 186

We're Already Married Chicken Meatballs 184

Meatballs 4 Ways

With endless flavor combinations and even a veg version thrown in, meatballs fill my husband Aaron's eyes with joy—one of life's truest delights. In the immortal words of the father of all meatballs, I would do anything for love.

Note: Whenever you're working with ground meat, keep it as cold as possible and avoid overmixing. This will ensure that the fat won't melt before it hits the heat of the oven, keeping everything nice and juicy and resulting in tender meatballs.

Every once in a while, a recipe will go viral that really has legs. There was that cucumber salad and that creamy chicken dish that was apparently so good, it would make anyone fall in love with you. With a love contract already firmly in place, I've put a spin on the dish to celebrate cozy nights in with my legally obligated lifelong guy.

We're Already Married Chicken Meatballs

SERVES 4

FOR THE MEATBALLS

1 teaspoon olive oil, plus more for drizzling

1 yellow onion, finely diced

Kosher salt

Freshly ground black pepper

1 garlic clove, minced

¼ cup breadcrumbs

¼ cup milk

1 egg

1 cup grated Parmigiano-Reggiano

2 tablespoons each chopped fresh parsley and basil

1 lb ground chicken

FOR THE SAUCE & SERVING

2 tablespoons butter

2 garlic cloves, minced

2 tablespoons all-purpose flour

2 tablespoons tomato paste

1 cup chicken broth (page 45 or store-bought)

1 cup whipping cream

½–1 cup grated Parmigiano-Reggiano

½–1 teaspoon crushed red pepper flakes

⅓ cup sliced sundried tomatoes

Kosher salt

Freshly ground black pepper

2 tablespoons each chopped fresh parsley and basil, for serving

Cooked pasta or crusty bread, for serving

For the meatballs, preheat your oven to 400°F and line a sheet pan with parchment paper.

Heat a high-sided sauté pan over medium heat and add the oil and onions. Season with salt and pepper and cook until lightly softened and golden, 2 to 3 minutes. Add the garlic and continue to cook for 30 seconds, then remove the pan from the heat and let cool.

Meanwhile, in a large mixing bowl, stir the breadcrumbs and milk together. Add the egg, Parmigiano-Reggiano, parsley, basil, and cooked onion mixture. Toss lightly to combine, then add the chicken and continue to gently toss and mix until evenly combined.

Using a spoon or small spring-loaded ice cream scoop, scoop small mounds (about 2 tablespoons) onto the prepared sheet pan. Drizzle with oil and lightly roll into meatballs. Roast the meatballs for 15 to 18 minutes, or until cooked to 165°F, then broil on high for 2 minutes for a little golden color on top. Set aside.

Meanwhile, prepare the sauce. Place the high-sided sauté pan back over medium heat and add the butter and garlic. Cook for 30 seconds, then whisk in the flour. Allow the flour to toast for 30 seconds to 1 minute, then whisk in the tomato paste. Cook for another 30 seconds to 1 minute, then slowly begin whisking in the chicken broth. Add the cream, bring to a simmer, and allow the sauce to bubble away until thickened, about 5 minutes. Stir in the cheese and red pepper flakes to taste, and sundried tomatoes, and season to taste with salt and pepper.

Stir in the cooked meatballs and scatter with the parsley and basil. Serve over your favorite pasta or with a few hunks of crusty bread.

AMORE
BACI

While Aaron is the main meatball lover in the house, Myra has never been able to say no to souvlaki. This recipe is perfect in a pita or on a Myra-preferred lettuce-y Greek salad, though the chunky orzo situation with homemade tzatziki is my preferred pairing.

Pork Souvlaki Meatballs

SERVES 4

FOR THE MEATBALLS

1 teaspoon olive oil, plus more for drizzling

1 small red onion, finely diced

Kosher salt

Freshly ground black pepper

1 garlic clove, minced

1½ teaspoons dried oregano

½ teaspoon ground cumin

½ teaspoon smoked paprika

½ teaspoon crushed red pepper flakes

¼ cup breadcrumbs

¼ cup milk

1 egg

3 tablespoons chopped fresh dill

2 tablespoons chopped fresh parsley

1 lemon, zested

1 lb ground pork

FOR THE ORZO

Kosher salt

1 cup orzo

1 lemon, zested and juiced

1 garlic clove, minced

½ red onion, thinly sliced

½ teaspoon dried oregano

¼ cup olive oil

Freshly ground black pepper

2 cups cherry tomatoes, halved

½ cucumber, diced

1 bell pepper, diced

For the meatballs, preheat your oven to 400°F and line a sheet pan with parchment paper.

Heat a high-sided sauté pan over medium heat and add the oil and onions. Season with salt and pepper and cook until lightly softened and golden, 2 to 3 minutes. Add the garlic, oregano, cumin, smoked paprika, and red pepper flakes and continue to cook for 30 seconds. Remove the pan from the heat and set aside to cool slightly or fully to room temperature.

Meanwhile, in a large mixing bowl, stir the breadcrumbs and milk together. Add the egg, dill, parsley, lemon zest, and cooked onion mixture. Toss to combine, then add the pork and continue to gently toss and mix until evenly combined.

Using a spoon or small spring-loaded ice cream scoop, scoop small mounds (about 2 tablespoons) onto the prepared sheet pan. Drizzle with oil and lightly roll into meatballs. Roast the meatballs for 15 to 18 minutes, or until cooked to 165°F, then broil on high for 2 minutes for a little golden color on top.

Meanwhile, for the orzo, bring a pot of water to a boil over high heat and season well with salt. Cook the orzo according to the package directions, then drain and rinse under cold water. Set aside.

In a large bowl, whisk together the lemon zest, lemon juice, garlic, onions, and oregano. Whisk in the oil and season with salt and pepper. Add the orzo, tomatoes, cucumbers, bell peppers, olives, feta, and dill and toss well to combine.

For the tzatziki, in a medium bowl, whisk together the yogurt, garlic, lemon zest, lemon juice, and olive oil. Grate the cucumber on the large side of a box grater and add to the yogurt mixture. Add the dill and parsley and season with salt and pepper.

Serve the meatballs over the orzo salad with tzatziki on the side.

½ cup pitted kalamata olives, whole or sliced

3½–5 oz crumbled feta

¼ cup chopped fresh dill

FOR THE TZATZIKI

1½ cups plain Greek yogurt

2 garlic cloves, minced

1 lemon, zested and juiced

2 tablespoons olive oil

½ cucumber, halved lengthwise and seeds removed

3–4 tablespoons chopped fresh dill

1 tablespoon chopped fresh parsley

Kosher salt

Freshly ground black pepper

Note: For a thicker tzatziki, grate the cucumber into a sieve and season with about 1 teaspoon of salt. Set the sieve over a bowl or in the sink and allow the cucumber to drain for about 20 minutes. Give the cucumber a good squeeze before adding to the yogurt mixture.

Spaghetti & Not Meatballs
Pork Souvlaki Meatballs

We're Already Married Chicken Meatballs
Salisbury Steak & Mushroom Meatballs

Calling a Salisbury steak a steak is a bit of a stretch. It is, at its base, a ground beef patty made famous by diners and microwavable TV dinners alike. Perhaps it's down to the fact that I haven't had a microwave for well over 10 years, but there is something so nostalgic about this classic dish. Smothered in mushroom gravy and served alongside mashed potatoes, these Salisbury steak–inspired meatballs make for a great dinner in front of the tube.

Salisbury Steak & Mushroom Meatballs

SERVES 4

FOR THE MEATBALLS

- 1 teaspoon olive oil, plus more for drizzling
- 1 small yellow onion, finely diced
- Kosher salt
- Freshly ground black pepper
- 1 garlic clove, minced
- 1 tablespoon Worcestershire sauce
- ¼ cup breadcrumbs
- ¼ cup beef broth
- 1 egg
- 2 teaspoons ketchup
- 1½ teaspoons Dijon mustard
- 1 lb lean ground beef

FOR THE GARLIC MASHED POTATOES

- 2¼ lb yellow potatoes, peeled and quartered
- 3 garlic cloves, peeled
- Kosher salt
- ¼ cup butter
- 1 cup buttermilk, milk, or cream

FOR THE SAUCE & SERVING

- 8 oz cremini mushrooms, sliced (see note)
- Kosher salt
- Freshly ground black pepper
- 2 tablespoons butter
- 1 yellow onion, finely diced

For the meatballs, preheat your oven to 400°F and line a sheet pan with parchment paper.

Heat a high-sided sauté pan over medium heat and add the oil and onions. Season with salt and pepper and cook until lightly softened and golden, 2 to 3 minutes. Add the garlic and Worcestershire sauce and continue to cook for 30 seconds. Remove the pan from the heat and set aside to cool slightly or fully to room temperature.

Meanwhile, in a large mixing bowl, stir the breadcrumbs and beef broth together. Add the egg, ketchup, Dijon, and cooked onion mixture, setting the sauté pan aside to use later for the sauce. Toss the breadcrumb mixture to combine, then add the beef and continue to gently toss and mix until evenly combined.

Using a spoon or small spring-loaded ice cream scoop, scoop small mounds (about 2 tablespoons) onto the prepared sheet pan. Drizzle with oil and lightly roll into meatballs. Roast the meatballs for 15 to 18 minutes, or until cooked to 165°F, then broil on high for 2 minutes for a little golden-brown color.

While the meatballs roast, make the garlic mashed potatoes. Place the potatoes and garlic in a large pot and cover with cold tap water. Season well with salt and bring to a boil over medium-high heat. Boil for 15 to 20 minutes, or until the potatoes are fork tender. Drain, then return the potatoes and garlic to the pot. Roughly mash with a potato masher and add the butter and whatever dairy you're using. Continue to mash or whip with a hand mixer if you like a smoother potato. Season well with salt, cover, and keep warm over low heat while you prepare the sauce.

For the sauce, place the sauté pan back over medium-high heat and add the mushrooms (see note). Season with salt and pepper and cook, stirring occasionally, for 5 to 6 minutes, or until lightly cooked down and golden. Turn the heat down to medium and add the butter and onions. Continue to cook for 3 to 4 minutes, until the onions are softened and golden. Stir in the garlic and cook for 30 seconds.

2 garlic cloves, minced
2 tablespoons all-purpose flour
2 cups beef broth
1 tablespoon Worcestershire sauce
1 teaspoon ketchup
1 teaspoon Dijon mustard
2 tablespoons chopped fresh parsley, for serving

Scatter in the flour, stir to combine, and allow the flour to toast for about 1 minute. Switch to a whisk and slowly begin whisking in the beef broth. Bring to a simmer and cook until thickened, about 3 minutes. Stir in the Worcestershire sauce, ketchup, and Dijon, then add the meatballs.

Serve the saucy meatballs over the mashed potatoes and scatter with the parsley.

Note: Mushrooms contain a ton of water and tend to steam. By cooking them in a dry pan first, you can cook off a good amount of that moisture before adding oil or butter. This gives them a better, meatier texture.

Trying to name this recipe wasn't easy. Neat balls? Gross. Veggie balls? Absolutely not. The more I tried, the more my mind wandered into the comedic territory of a 12-year-old. Thus, I give you "not meatballs."

Spaghetti & Not Meatballs

SERVES 4

FOR THE NOT MEATBALLS

½ cup chopped walnuts

Olive oil

1 small yellow onion, finely diced

Kosher salt

Freshly ground black pepper

2 cups roughly chopped mushrooms

3 garlic cloves, finely minced

1 tablespoon soy sauce

1 teaspoon balsamic vinegar

1½ cups canned lentils

½ cup ground Parmigiano-Reggiano

2 tablespoons chopped fresh parsley

2 tablespoons chopped fresh basil

1 tablespoon chopped fresh oregano

FOR THE SAUCE, SPAGHETTI & SERVING

2 tablespoons olive oil

2 garlic cloves, thinly sliced

½–1 teaspoon crushed red pepper flakes, optional

Kosher salt

1 can (28 fl oz) crushed tomatoes

9 oz spaghetti

2 tablespoons chopped fresh parsley

2 tablespoons chopped fresh basil

2 teaspoons chopped fresh oregano

Ground Parmigiano-Reggiano, for serving

For the not meatballs, in a large dry nonstick skillet, toast the walnuts over medium heat, stirring often, for 2 minutes, or until they begin to smell nutty. Transfer the walnuts to the bowl of your food processor and set aside. Place the skillet back onto the heat and add 1 tablespoon of olive oil and the onions. Season with salt and pepper and cook for 3 minutes, or until the onions are softened and lightly golden brown, then add the chopped mushrooms. Season with more salt and pepper and allow the mushrooms to cook down for 6 to 8 minutes, stirring occasionally. Add the garlic and cook for another 30 seconds.

Deglaze the pan with the soy sauce and balsamic vinegar and cook, stirring constantly, until the liquid has evaporated. Transfer the mushroom mixture to the food processor and add the lentils, Parmigiano-Reggiano, parsley, basil, and oregano. Pulse six to eight times to chop everything up and bring the mixture together, being careful not to make a smooth puree. Season to taste with more salt and pepper, if needed.

Using a spring-loaded ice cream scoop or a spoon, divide the mixture into sixteen equal portions and roll into meatballs (see note).

Turn the heat under the skillet to medium-high and add about 1 tablespoon of olive oil. Fry the meatballs in batches until golden on both sides, 3 to 4 minutes per side, adding more oil as needed. The meatballs will be quite tender and may be tricky to flip. If they break apart, just smooth them back together and continue frying. Set the meatballs aside on a sheet pan while you prepare the sauce.

For the sauce, turn the heat under the skillet down to medium and add the oil, garlic, and red pepper flakes, if using. Season with salt and cook for 30 seconds, just until the garlic has softened. Carefully pour in the crushed tomatoes (things will splatter!), cover the pan with a slightly off-kilter lid, and turn the heat down to medium-low to simmer.

Meanwhile, cook the spaghetti. Place a large pot of water over high heat and bring to a boil. Season well with salt and cook the spaghetti according to the package directions.

When the spaghetti is almost cooked, add the parsley, basil, and oregano to the sauce along with the meatballs to heat through.

Serve the spaghetti topped with the sauce and meatballs, along with a good helping of ground Parmigiano-Reggiano.

Note: When shaping things like burgers, meatballs, or even arancini, lightly dampen your hands with tap water before rolling to stop the mixture from sticking to your fingers.

Good times

True to form, my university years really expanded my knowledge of late-night cuisine. Sure, there were the normal nights of pizza and poutine, but right across from campus was this Mediterranean spot that was open late, slinging everyone's favorite gyros. They were spicy, saucy, and the perfect thing to grab after a concert. This is my homemade homage to those late-night wraps. By schmearing the filling over the pita, as you would when making lahmacun, you'll get goodness in every single bite.

Late-Night Smash Wrap

SERVES 4

FOR THE PITAS

4 oz feta or halloumi
1 lb ground pork or chicken
1 teaspoon ground cumin
1 teaspoon ground coriander
½ teaspoon garlic powder
½ teaspoon smoked paprika
½ teaspoon dried oregano
½ teaspoon crushed red pepper flakes
Kosher salt
Freshly ground black pepper
4 Greek pitas
Olive oil

FOR THE TOPPINGS

1 cup plain Greek yogurt
1 lemon, halved, divided
2 garlic cloves, minced
2 tablespoons finely chopped fresh dill, mint, and parsley
Kosher salt
Freshly ground black pepper
Olive oil
½ red onion, thinly sliced
½ cucumber, diced or thinly sliced
½ teaspoon dried oregano
1 cup cherry tomatoes, halved or quartered
1 romaine heart, chopped or shredded
2 oz feta or halloumi

For the pitas, preheat your oven to 200°F and set out a sheet pan.

Crumble the feta or grate the halloumi on the large side of a box grater. Transfer to a large bowl along with the ground meat, cumin, coriander, garlic powder, smoked paprika, oregano, and red pepper flakes. Season with a little salt (not too much as, no matter which you use, the cheese is salty) and pepper.

Heat a large cast-iron or nonstick skillet over medium-high heat. Lay out the pitas and divide the meat mixture evenly among them. Using the back of a spoon or an offset spatula, spread the meat mixture into an even layer across the surface of the pitas. The cheese might make a perfectly even layer impossible, but don't worry—you just want to spread it as evenly as you can. Drizzle a little oil into the pan and fry the pitas in batches, meat side down, until the meat is well caramelized and cooked through, 4 to 5 minutes. Transfer to the sheet pan, meat side up, and place in the oven to keep warm while you fry the rest of the pitas and prepare the toppings.

For the toppings, in a small bowl, combine the yogurt with the zest and juice of half the lemon. Add the garlic, dill, mint, and parsley and season with a little salt and pepper. Drizzle in 1 tablespoon of olive oil, if you'd like, and stir well to combine.

In a large bowl, toss the onions and cucumbers with the juice from the remaining lemon half and season with the oregano and some salt and pepper. Use your hand or a pair of tongs to scrunch the veg up a bit and lightly break them down. Add the tomatoes and lettuce along with 1 tablespoon of olive oil and toss to combine.

To serve, retrieve the pitas from the oven, drizzle with the yogurt sauce, top with the veg salad, and scatter with crumbled feta or grated halloumi.

The kitchen has always been my happy place, but when I switched careers to food TV and recipe writing, I was worried that might change. Taking something that was always a creative hobby and turning it into work can sometimes sour things, but luckily that didn't happen for me. I still find joy every time I step up to the stove and am absolutely thrilled to the gills when I figure out a new way to make something delicious. Case in point: When I figured out how to make breaded things not only simpler but also more delicious, I wanted to shout it from the rooftops. The sneaky addition of mayonnaise to an egg wash gives you my signature "food gloop," which eliminates the need to dredge things in flour and helps even more crispies stick to the surface.

Pork Schnitz with Vinegary Slaw

SERVES 4

FOR THE SLAW

1 lemon, halved, divided
3 tablespoons white vinegar
1½ teaspoons Dijon mustard
1 teaspoon sugar
¼ cup canola or olive oil
Kosher salt or celery salt
Freshly ground black pepper
½ small red onion, thinly sliced
¼ green cabbage, shredded
1 cup thinly sliced cucumbers

FOR THE SCHNITZEL

4 boneless pork chops
Kosher salt
Freshly ground black pepper
Canola oil
2 eggs
3 tablespoons mayonnaise
1 tablespoon Dijon mustard
1 teaspoon garlic powder
2 cups panko breadcrumbs

For the slaw, in a large bowl, combine the juice of half the lemon, vinegar, mustard, and sugar. Whisk in the oil, season with salt and pepper, and toss in the onions, cabbage, and cucumbers. Set aside at room temperature to lightly pickle while you prepare the schnitzel.

For the schnitzel, preheat your oven to 200°F and line a sheet pan with a cooling rack.

Working with one pork chop at a time, cover with a piece of parchment paper or plastic wrap and use a meat mallet, heavy-bottomed skillet, or rolling pin to pound the chop to a scant ½ inch thick. Season both sides with salt and pepper and set aside.

Place a large cast-iron skillet or heavy-bottomed sauté pan over medium heat and add ½ inch of oil.

Set out two shallow dishes. In the first, beat together the eggs, mayonnaise, mustard, and garlic powder. Place the panko in the second dish and season with salt and pepper.

Working with one chop at a time, dunk in the egg mixture and then press the chop into the panko to evenly coat.

Working in batches to avoid overcrowding the pan, fry the chops for 3 to 4 minutes per side, or until golden and cooked through. Transfer to the cooling rack, season immediately with salt, and place in the oven to keep warm while you fry the rest.

Serve the schnitzel with the pickled slaw and the remaining lemon half cut into wedges on the side.

When Aaron and I first started dating, I figured out early on that the way to his heart was pie. Specifically hand pies. When you think about it, sausage rolls are essentially savory hand pies and make for the perfect packable love note to wrap up and send for lunch.

The Perfect Lunch, a.k.a. Sausage Rolls

SERVES 4 TO 6

FOR THE SAUSAGE ROLLS

1 sheet frozen puff pastry

2 oz thinly sliced pancetta, finely diced

1 tablespoon butter or oil

1 shallot, finely minced

Kosher salt

Freshly ground black pepper

1 tablespoon brandy, optional

1 tablespoon maple syrup

1 lb ground pork

¼ cup breadcrumbs

2 garlic cloves, minced

1 tablespoon finely chopped fresh sage

2 teaspoons finely chopped fresh rosemary

1 teaspoon smoked paprika

1 egg

1 tablespoon water

2 tablespoons Dijon mustard

1 tablespoon sesame seeds

FOR THE DIP

½ cup mayonnaise

¼ cup Dijon mustard

½ teaspoon smoked paprika

2–3 tablespoons maple syrup

For the sausage rolls, thaw the puff pastry according to the package directions.

When the pastry is thawed, place your oven rack in the lowest position and preheat the oven to 400°F. Line a sheet pan with parchment paper and set aside.

Place a skillet over medium heat and add the pancetta, butter or oil, and shallots. Season with salt and pepper and cook until the pancetta is crisp and the shallots are softened, 2 to 3 minutes. Deglaze the pan with brandy, if using, and stir in the maple syrup. Transfer to a large bowl to cool to room temperature.

When cool, add the pork, breadcrumbs, garlic, sage, rosemary, and smoked paprika and season with ½ teaspoon each of salt and pepper.

Unroll the sheet of puff pastry and cut it in half so that you have two long rectangles. In a small bowl, beat the egg and water together to make an egg wash, and set aside.

Spread the Dijon lengthwise down the center of each piece of pastry. Using your hands, divide the pork mixture in half and shape into two sausages roughly the same length as the puff pastry. Working with one piece of pastry at a time, place a sausage on top of the mustard and brush one long edge of the pastry with a little egg wash. Fold and roll the pastry over the sausage and arrange seam side down on the parchment-lined sheet pan.

Using a sharp knife, cut each log into two or three equal portions, slash a small vent in the top of each, and brush with egg wash. Scatter with a pinch of salt and some sesame seeds. Bake for 30 to 35 minutes, or until the pastry is deeply golden brown and the sausage is cooked through.

Meanwhile, make the dip. In a small bowl, whisk the mayonnaise, mustard, smoked paprika, and maple syrup to taste.

Serve the sausage rolls hot with the dip, or chill both in the fridge for the perfect grab-and-go lunch.

A few years back, I had the opportunity to lean into a holiday. My last cookbook was headed to the printer, I was about to start another round of my cooking show, and I realized that I had a span of about 4 weeks where, for the first time in 8 years, I had nothing on the docket. Aaron and I packed our bags and headed for the Tuscan hills. It was the middle of January, and after a harrowing drive in the dark from Rome to Florence, we awoke on our first morning to the sun shining through our windows and a dusting of snow covering the ground. While Aaron and I enjoyed cappuccinos in bed, all seemed calm . . . until we heard the blast of a shotgun. It wasn't until a few days later that we learned we had arrived at the tail end of boar hunting season. While boar is a traditional staple in Tuscan cuisine, it's a bit tricky to come by here in Toronto, so its less hairy cousin will have to do.

Pork Ragu

MAKES ABOUT 8 CUPS

- 2 tablespoons olive oil
- 1 lb pork shoulder, cut into 2-inch chunks
- Kosher salt
- Freshly ground black pepper
- 2 yellow onions
- 2 carrots
- 2 celery stalks
- 1 small fennel bulb
- 1–2 sprigs fresh rosemary
- 2 teaspoons fennel seeds
- 2 garlic cloves, minced
- 1 cup dry white wine
- 2 cans (13 fl oz each) cherry tomatoes or 1 can (28 fl oz) whole tomatoes
- ½–1 cup chicken broth (page 45 or store-bought)

FOR SERVING

- Soft polenta (page 125) or pasta of your choice
- Finely grated pecorino Romano

Heat a Dutch oven over medium-high heat and add the oil.

Dry the pork with some paper towel and season well with salt and pepper. Sear the pork until golden brown, working in batches if necessary, 2 to 3 minutes per side, then set aside.

Using a knife or a food processor, very finely dice the onions, carrots, celery, and fennel and add to the pan along with the rosemary and fennel seeds. Season with salt and pepper, turn the heat down to medium-low, and cook for about 15 minutes, stirring occasionally, until soft. You do not want the vegetables to caramelize much, so watch the temperature.

Once soft, adjust the heat to medium-high and stir in the garlic. Deglaze the pan with the white wine and allow the wine to reduce slightly for about 1 minute. Add the canned tomatoes and, using a spoon, lightly crush the tomatoes against the side of the pan. Add the pork back to the pan along with any juices that have collected and pour in enough chicken broth to cover the pork. Bring the mixture to a boil, then cover the pot with a tight-fitting lid and turn the heat down to low to maintain a gentle simmer. Simmer the sauce for 2 to 2½ hours, or until the pork is tender and easily shreds with a fork.

Remove the pork from the sauce and set aside in a bowl or shallow dish. Using two forks, finely shred the pork. Discard the rosemary sprig(s) and return the pork to the sauce. Season to taste with salt and pepper. If desired, simmer the sauce uncovered for a thicker consistency.

Serve immediately over soft polenta (see the Creamy Mushrooms with Polenta on page 125) or your favorite cooked pasta with lots of pecorino Romano. You can also transfer to sealable containers and cool to room temperature before storing in the fridge for up to 3 days or in the freezer for up to 3 months.

If you're more of a beef ragu family, swap out the pork for stewing beef.

Note: There's no shame in a store-bought pickle! My preference for a burger is always a chip (a.k.a. a round slice), but long slices will do just fine.

Everyone needs a good burger recipe, and I've gone on quite the journey to find my family's go-to. Sure, a jazzed-up patty has its place, but when a burger lover in our house wants a burger, they usually want something straightforward and almost fast-food-y. This is a smash burger at its finest, but don't skip on the saucy iceberg lettuce. It's a total game changer.

Onion Smash Burgers with Sweet & Sour Pickles

SERVES 2 TO 4 (WITH LEFTOVER PICKLES)

FOR THE PICKLES

4 mini cucumbers, thinly sliced
¼ white onion, thinly sliced
1 tablespoon kosher salt
¼ cup dark brown sugar, packed
¼ cup white or cider vinegar
2 tablespoons water
2 teaspoons yellow mustard
1 teaspoon mustard seeds
1 teaspoon celery salt

FOR THE SAUCE

¼ cup mayonnaise
2 tablespoons ketchup
1 tablespoon relish
1 teaspoon yellow mustard
½ teaspoon white vinegar
½ teaspoon sugar

FOR THE BURGERS

1 lb lean ground beef
Kosher salt
Freshly ground black pepper
Canola oil
½ small white onion, finely diced
2 tablespoons yellow mustard
4 slices medium cheddar
2–4 burger buns
2 cups finely shredded iceberg lettuce
Sliced tomato

For the pickles, add the cucumbers, onions, and salt to a small bowl. Scrunch the veg up a bit and set aside for 30 minutes to allow the salt to draw out some of the moisture and soften the veg.

Meanwhile, in a small pot or microwave-safe dish, combine the sugar, vinegar, and water. Add the mustard, mustard seeds, and celery salt and heat over medium or in the microwave until the mixture is hot and the sugar has dissolved. Set aside to cool slightly.

Transfer the cucumbers and onions to a sieve and rinse under cold water to remove the salt. Gently squeeze the veg to remove as much water as possible, then transfer to a clean glass jar or container. Pour the pickling liquid overtop, topping it off with a splash of water or vinegar if needed to cover the veg. Set aside to cool to room temperature, then seal and let pickle in the fridge for at least 1 day or up to 2 weeks.

For the sauce, whisk together the mayonnaise, ketchup, relish, mustard, vinegar, and sugar and set aside.

For the burgers, heat a large cast-iron skillet over high heat. Divide the beef into four equal portions and shape each into a ball. Season well with salt and pepper. Add a small splash of oil to the pan and add the beef. Lightly press the burgers down with a spatula to flatten slightly, then scatter the top of each with some diced onions. Firmly press the burgers down until quite flat and cook for 3 to 4 minutes, or until well seared.

Flip the burgers over and brush the seared side with mustard. Continue to cook the burgers for 2 minutes, or until cooked through. Add a slice of cheese to each, cover the pan, remove it from the heat, and allow the cheese to melt. Once melted, remove the burgers from the pan, and set aside to rest for 1 to 2 minutes while you prepare the buns and toppings.

Toast the buns, if desired, and toss the lettuce with a few tablespoons of the prepared sauce. Add the lettuce to the bottom buns, top with one to two patties, then garnish with a few sweet and sour pickles, a tomato slice, and extra sauce.

These shredded beef tacos combine homemade deliciousness with the from-a-box textures and flavors you know and love. If I do say so myself, this is a major upgrade to the already pretty perfect taco kit.

Shredded Beef Tacos

SERVES 4

FOR THE BEEF

1½–2 lb chuck or sirloin tip roast
1 tablespoon all-purpose flour
2 teaspoons chili powder
1 teaspoon ground cumin
1 teaspoon garlic powder
1 teaspoon smoked paprika
½ teaspoon onion powder
½ teaspoon kosher salt
¼ teaspoon freshly ground black pepper
2 teaspoons canola oil
1 onion, thinly sliced
2 garlic cloves, finely chopped
½ cup light-flavored beer
1 tablespoon Worcestershire sauce
2 cups low-sodium beef broth, plus more if needed

FOR THE TACOS

12–16 soft corn or flour tortillas
Canola oil
1 romaine heart, shredded
2 tomatoes, diced
5–7 oz cheddar, grated
Sour cream
Salsa or pico de gallo
Guacamole

Preheat your oven to 300°F.

For the beef, place a Dutch oven over medium-high heat and dry the roast with paper towel. In a small bowl, combine the flour, chili powder, cumin, garlic powder, smoked paprika, onion powder, salt, and pepper. Evenly scatter the seasoned flour over the beef (you may have some leftover), pressing to adhere. Add the oil to the pot and sear the beef until golden brown all over, 3 to 5 minutes per side. Remove the beef to a rimmed sheet pan or large bowl to catch any juices and set aside.

Turn the heat down to medium, add the onions, season with salt and pepper, and cook for 3 to 5 minutes, stirring occasionally, just until the onions pick up a little color. Stir in the garlic and any remaining seasoned flour, cook for 30 seconds, then deglaze the pan with the beer and Worcestershire sauce, scraping the bottom to remove any stuck-on bits.

Put the beef back in the pot and pour in enough broth to come halfway up the side of the beef. Bring to a simmer, then cover with a tight-fitting lid and transfer to the oven for 2 to 2½ hours, or until the roast is fork tender. Set the roast aside for 15 minutes to rest. Increase the oven temperature to 375°F.

For the tacos, if your tortillas are stiff, wrap them in a damp kitchen towel and heat in the microwave for 15 seconds or in the oven for 1 to 2 minutes. Brush both sides of the tortillas with a little canola oil to coat. Pull an oven rack out and carefully drape the tortillas over two bars so they form an upside-down taco shell shape. Bake for 8 to 10 minutes, or until crisp and golden brown. Carefully transfer the shells to a serving platter. Prepare and set out the toppings.

Once the meat has rested, transfer it to a large bowl or serving dish. Using two forks, shred the beef. Spoon over as much of the braising liquid as you'd like and serve any remainder on the side along with the crispy shells and toppings.

Note: If soft taco shells are more your bag, simply warm corn or flour tortillas in a pan over high heat.

In my experience, the easiest people to cook for are meat lovers. With a bit of salt and pepper and a good amount of heat, a basic steak is all you need to bring a big smile to their faces. By adding a few flavor boosters, this simple version of steak au poivre will have them grinning from ear to ear.

Steak with Brandy Peppercorn Sauce

SERVES 4

- Two 1-inch-thick boneless rib eye or striploin steaks
- Kosher salt
- Freshly ground black pepper
- 1 tablespoon olive oil
- 2 sprigs fresh rosemary or sage
- 3 garlic cloves, divided
- 2 tablespoons butter
- 1 shallot, finely diced
- 2 teaspoons coarsely cracked black pepper
- ¼ cup brandy
- ⅔ cup whipping cream
- 1 tablespoon grainy or stone-ground Dijon mustard

About 2 hours before you're ready to cook, remove the steaks from the fridge and set on a rack-lined sheet pan. Season well with salt and set aside.

When you're ready to cook, preheat your oven to 250°F and insert a leave-in digital probe thermometer through the side of one of the steaks (see note).

Dry the steaks with a few pieces of paper towel, then season with salt and pepper. Cook the steaks in the low oven until the internal temperature reaches 115°F for medium-rare (about 25 to 30 minutes).

When the steaks are almost up to temperature, heat a cast-iron or stainless-steel skillet over high heat. Remove the steaks from the oven, drizzle with oil, and add to the hot pan along with the rosemary or sage and two garlic cloves. Sear the steaks for 2 to 3 minutes total, flipping occasionally, or until deeply golden on both sides and the internal temperature reaches 135°F for medium-rare.

Remove the steaks, rosemary, and garlic from the pan and tent with aluminum foil. Set aside while you prepare the sauce.

Turn the heat off under the pan and add the butter to melt. Thinly slice the remaining garlic clove and add to the pan along with the shallots. Season with salt and the coarsely cracked pepper and cook for 1 to 2 minutes, or until lightly golden. At this point, the residual heat from the pan should be enough to cook the shallots and garlic. Carefully add the brandy, standing back in case of any flare-ups, and turn the heat under the pan to medium. Cook for 1 minute to allow the brandy to almost fully evaporate, then stir in the cream and mustard and simmer for 1 minute, or until slightly thickened. Season to taste with salt.

Thickly slice the steak and serve with the peppery cream sauce spooned overtop.

Note: I'm not much of a gadget gal, but when it comes to purchasing and preparing a pricey cut of meat like a thick-cut steak, a leave-in digital probe thermometer is a must. Not to sound too much like an infomercial, but it's a one-time investment that will ensure a perfect steak (or chicken, turkey, or roast pork) every single time.

Li'l Sweeties

Treat. Yo. Self.

For someone who loves to bake, I feel like I need to come clean. I don't love super sugary sweet treats. Perhaps this is the world's worst kept secret, but if you've baked any of my recipes before, you may have noticed that I tend to lean more sour, salty, nutty, or, at most, fruity. These bars take the last three and bring them together for some lunchbox nostalgia.

PB&J Bars

MAKES 16

- ¾ cup butter, room temperature
- ¾ cup dark brown sugar, packed
- 1 egg
- ½ teaspoon vanilla extract
- 1 cup rolled oats
- 1 cup all-purpose flour
- ½ teaspoon baking powder
- ½ teaspoon cinnamon
- ¼ teaspoon kosher salt
- ½ cup chopped peanuts
- 1½–2 cups jam, any flavor

Preheat your oven to 350°F and lightly grease a 9-inch square baking pan with nonstick cooking spray. Line the pan with a sling of parchment paper.

In a large bowl, cream the butter and brown sugar until well combined. Beat in the egg and vanilla and set aside.

Add the oats to your food processor and pulse, eight to ten times, until finely ground. Add the flour, baking powder, cinnamon, and salt and pulse to combine. Add the peanuts and pulse three to four more times to combine and further chop the peanuts.

Add the dry ingredients to the butter mixture and stir just until combined.

Transfer about three-quarters of the dough to the prepared pan. Using your hands or a rubber spatula, spread and press the mixture into the bottom of the pan. Spoon the jam onto the crust and carefully spread it into an even layer. Tear and dollop the remaining dough over the jam.

Bake for 35 to 40 minutes, or until golden brown. The jam might be quite fluid at this point, but it will set up upon cooling.

Allow to cool to room temperature, then cut into bars. Store in an airtight container at room temperature for up to 4 days.

Note: With rolled oats, peanuts, and whatever jam's your jam, these bars can easily double as a quick grab-and-go breakfast.

This recipe goes out to one of the amazing producers I have the pleasure of working with. She has been trying to get me to make some sort of lemon meringue cookie pretty much since I met her, so this one goes out to the one and only CharChar Binks.

Lemon Almond Meringue Cookies

MAKES 20

1 cup butter, room temperature
¾ cup sugar
1 teaspoon vanilla extract
½ teaspoon almond extract
1 egg white
2 cups all-purpose flour
¾ cup almond flour
2 teaspoons cornstarch
1 teaspoon kosher salt
¼ teaspoon baking soda
1½ cups marshmallow crème, such as Fluff
1½ cups lemon curd (page 213 or store-bought)

In a large bowl or the bowl of your stand mixer fitted with the paddle attachment, cream the butter and sugar until light and fluffy, about 2 minutes. Add the vanilla and almond extracts and the egg white and beat well to combine.

In a separate bowl, whisk together the flour, almond flour, cornstarch, salt, and baking soda. Add the dry ingredients to the butter mixture and stir just until combined.

Line a sheet pan with parchment paper. Scoop the dough into about ¼-cup mounds, place them on the sheet pan, and roll each into a ball. At this point, the cookie dough balls can be touching. Transfer to the fridge to chill for at least 30 minutes to allow the butter to firm up and the flour to hydrate.

Meanwhile, preheat your oven to 350°F and line two more large sheet pans with parchment paper.

Place the chilled cookie dough balls onto the prepared sheet pans, leaving a few inches of space between each. Bake the cookies for 14 to 16 minutes, or until lightly golden around the edges and set, rotating the pans if needed. Transfer to a rack and cool completely to room temperature. Cooled cookies can be stored in an airtight container at room temperature for up to 5 days and decorated just before digging in.

When ready to serve, transfer the marshmallow crème to a piping bag or a zip-top bag with the corner cut off and pipe a circle onto each cookie. Using a kitchen torch, lightly toast the marshmallow. Alternatively, you can lightly broil the meringue-topped cookies on high until golden, about 30 seconds to 1 minute. Dollop the lemon curd in the center of the cookies and enjoy today.

Note: If you're looking to get ahead or if you don't want to bake off all the cookies at once, transfer the cookie dough balls (still on the pan) to the freezer. Once frozen, transfer to a zip-top freezer bag and store in the freezer for up to 3 months. Bake from frozen at 350°F for 16 to 18 minutes.

Simple Lemon Curd

- 1 tablespoon lemon zest (about 1 lemon)
- ½ cup lemon juice (about 3 lemons)
- ½ cup sugar
- ¼ teaspoon kosher salt
- 3 eggs
- ¼ teaspoon almond extract
- 1 tablespoon butter

In a small saucepot, whisk the lemon zest, lemon juice, sugar, salt, and eggs and cook over medium heat, stirring often, until thick, 2 to 4 minutes. Whisk in the almond extract and butter and remove the curd from the heat. Pass it through a fine-mesh sieve, transfer to a resealable container, and chill completely in the fridge. Lemon curd will last in the fridge for up to 1 week.

Remember the joy of being a kid when the bell rang and you ran to get your lunch bag, frantically unpacking it to see what Chef Mom or Chef Dad packed that day? For me, there was nothing more exciting than seeing the glint of a pudding cup, specifically rice pudding. I know, it's probably the most grandpa pudding preference out there, but it's delicious! You can keep the raisin variety for yourself, because I'm going to be digging into this indisputably better flavor combination.

Orange Cinnamon Brûléed Rice Pudding

SERVES 4

1 tablespoon butter
½ cup arborio rice
2 cups whole milk
4 tablespoons sugar, divided
⅛ teaspoon kosher salt
½ cup whipping cream
½ orange, zested
¼ teaspoon cinnamon
½ teaspoon vanilla extract or 1 teaspoon vanilla bean paste
1 egg yolk

In a large saucepan over medium heat, melt the butter. Add the rice and toast for about 1 minute. Add the milk, 2 tablespoons of sugar, and the salt, and bring to a light boil. Turn the heat down to medium-low and cook, stirring often, until the rice is tender and the mixture has thickened, 15 to 20 minutes.

Meanwhile, whisk together the whipping cream, orange zest, cinnamon, vanilla, and egg yolk. Once the rice is tender, add about ½ cup of the hot rice mixture to the cream mixture and whisk to combine. Whisk in another ½ cup to temper the cream, then pour the mixture into the pot.

Turn the heat down to low and cook, stirring constantly, until the rice pudding is thick enough to coat the back of a spoon, about 5 minutes.

Divide the rice pudding among four shallow heatproof ramekins or bowls and scatter the remaining 2 tablespoons of sugar evenly overtop of all. Using a kitchen torch, torch the sugary surface until melted and golden brown. Alternatively, you can broil the puddings on high in the top third of your oven for 2 to 4 minutes, or until the sugar is golden brown.

Serve immediately.

Note: Like with any brûléed dessert, the sugary top will lose its crunch and texture pretty quickly, but that's OK. You'll still get the smoky caramel flavor in every bite.

As an early birthday present to my mom, Aaron and I took her to Scotland for Christmas holidays. After a jaunt in Edinburgh, we settled in Pittenweem, a seaside fishing village equipped with a great little spot just up the wynd called the West End Bar. We quickly became regulars, and after an ultra comforting Christmas Eve meal of the best fish and chips, we were stuffed to the gills. The only thing to tempt our fancy? This ultra lemony citrus-set dessert.

Lemon Posset

SERVES 8

- 2 cups whipping cream
- ½ cup sugar
- ⅛ teaspoon kosher salt
- 2–3 lemons, divided
- ¼ teaspoon vanilla extract

Pour the whipping cream into a large saucepan, then stir in the sugar, salt, and the zest of two lemons. Place the saucepan over medium-high heat and bring to a boil. Boil for 10 minutes to dissolve the sugar and reduce the cream slightly, stirring often and adjusting the heat as needed, keeping an eye on the cream to make sure it doesn't boil over.

Meanwhile, squeeze ⅓ cup of lemon juice and set aside.

Remove the saucepan from the heat and immediately whisk in the lemon juice and vanilla. Pour the mixture through a fine-mesh sieve into a spouted measuring cup, then portion it into eight serving cups.

Leaving the lemon possets uncovered, chill in the fridge for 4 hours to set up. Once set, you can serve them or cover them and refrigerate for up to 1 week or freeze for up to 3 months. If frozen, temper the possets in the fridge for 1 to 2 hours before serving.

If there is one thing I love, it's anthropomorphizing food. From loudly proclaiming "GIRRRL!" to any dish that really wows, to giving full personalities to certain ingredients, there's just something about making a dish feel like an old pal that brings me comfort. Take, for instance, molasses. An old standby and one of my favorite deeply flavored sweeteners, molasses, in my mind takes the form of an old man in a tweed suit, hat at a jaunty angle and glasses on the end of his nose, with a sweet little twinkle in his eye.

Ginger Carrot Loaf

MAKES 1 STANDARD LOAF

1¾ cups all-purpose flour
2 teaspoons ground ginger
1 teaspoon ground cinnamon
¼ teaspoon ground cloves
¼ teaspoon freshly grated nutmeg
½ teaspoon baking powder
½ teaspoon baking soda
¼ teaspoon kosher salt
⅓ cup vegetable oil
¾ cup sugar
½ cup molasses
½ teaspoon vanilla extract
2 eggs
2 medium carrots, grated
¾ cup apple juice or water

Preheat your oven to 350°F and lightly grease a standard 9-by-5-inch loaf pan with nonstick cooking spray.

In a large bowl, whisk together the flour, ginger, cinnamon, cloves, nutmeg, baking powder, baking soda, and salt.

In a separate bowl, beat together the oil, sugar, molasses, vanilla, and eggs. Stir in the grated carrots and juice or water. Add the wet mixture to the dry ingredients and whisk just to combine, scraping down the bowl a few times to ensure that everything is evenly mixed.

Pour the batter into the prepared pan and bake for 55 minutes to 1 hour, or until deeply golden brown and a cake tester or skewer inserted in the center of the loaf comes out clean.

Allow the loaf to cool in the pan for at least 20 minutes before turning it out onto a wire rack to cool slightly or all the way to room temperature.

Serve the loaf as is, warm with butter for a snack, or with a scoop of ice cream for dessert. Cool and store at room temperature in an airtight container for up to 1 week.

Note: Molasses is one of my all-time favorite flavors and is something I always have on hand in my pantry. But if you're wary of buying a carton only to have it sit forgotten in your cupboard for the next 5 years, have no fear! It's great to have around in case you need brown sugar in a pinch. Simply blitz 1 cup of white sugar with 1 tablespoon of molasses for light brown sugar or with 2 tablespoons for dark.

One of my favorite things about baking is, no matter how often you do it, it can always feel like an experiment. Whether it's using a common substitute like milk and vinegar in place of buttermilk or switching up cake flour with all-purpose and a sprinkle of cornstarch, it often just takes a little know-how to make do with what you have on hand. A few years ago, I roguishly tossed some cookie crumbs into a cake batter to make up for a scant measurement of flour, and I was thrilled to the gills with the results. Not only do cookie crumbs act similarly to flour in smaller doses, they add a little extra texture and tons of flavor to the result. This snack cake gets a double dose of ginger flavor thanks to the spice itself and those delish little crumbs.

Apple Ginger Snack Cake

MAKES ONE 9-INCH SQUARE CAKE

FOR THE CAKE

½ cup unsalted butter
⅔ cup dark brown sugar, packed
2 eggs
1 teaspoon vanilla extract
2 cups grated firm apple, such as Granny Smith
1¾ oz (about 4) store-bought gingersnaps or graham crackers
1 cup all-purpose flour
½ cup whole wheat flour
1 teaspoon ground cinnamon
½ teaspoon ground ginger
¼ teaspoon freshly grated nutmeg
1 teaspoon baking powder
½ teaspoon baking soda
½ teaspoon kosher salt
½ cup chopped walnuts

FOR THE FROSTING

1 cup brick-style cream cheese, room temperature
½ cup icing sugar
1 teaspoon vanilla extract
½ teaspoon ground cinnamon
Pinch ground ginger

For the cake, preheat your oven to 350°F and lightly grease a 9-inch square baking pan with nonstick cooking spray.

In a small saucepan over medium heat, melt the butter. Allow the butter to foam up and brown, stirring often. This should take 4 to 5 minutes. Transfer the butter to a large bowl and set aside to cool.

Add the sugar to the butter and beat well until the mixture is a little lighter in color. Beat in the eggs, one at a time, then stir in the vanilla and grated apple. Set aside.

Place the gingersnaps in a heavy-duty plastic bag and smash into very fine crumbs. Transfer the crumbs to a medium bowl and whisk in the flours, cinnamon, ginger, nutmeg, baking powder, baking soda, and salt. Add the dry ingredients to the wet and stir just until almost combined. Fold in the walnuts.

Transfer the batter to the prepared pan and bake for 30 to 35 minutes, or until the cake has risen and a toothpick inserted in the center comes out clean. Set aside to cool completely.

Meanwhile, make the frosting. In a bowl, beat the cream cheese and icing sugar together. Stir in the vanilla, cinnamon, and ginger to taste, and spread or pipe over the cake.

Store the cake in an airtight container in the fridge for up to 5 days. For optimal texture, remove the cake from the fridge 30 minutes before serving.

Note: This batter is quite thick, almost like a blondie or brownie batter, but thanks to the additional moisture from the apple, it bakes up tender like a cake.

There are times in life that simply demand certain types of food. There's chicken soup for when you're feeling under the weather, buttery popcorn for when you're extra stressed, and ice cream for when some jabroni pulls a fast one.

Chocolate Peanut Butter No-Churn Ice Cream

MAKES ABOUT 5 CUPS

- 1 can (10 fl oz) sweetened condensed milk
- ⅓ cup cocoa powder
- 1½ teaspoons vanilla extract
- ¼ teaspoon kosher salt
- 2 cups whipping cream
- ½ cup chopped peanuts
- 6 chocolate peanut butter cups, chopped (see note)

Place a standard 9-by-5-inch loaf pan in the freezer.

In a large bowl, whisk together the sweetened condensed milk, cocoa powder, vanilla, and salt, and set aside.

In a separate bowl or in the bowl of your stand mixer fitted with the whisk attachment, whip the cream on medium speed to stiff peaks, 2 to 3 minutes.

Using a silicone spatula, gently fold one-third of the whipped cream into the condensed milk mixture. Fold the remaining whipped cream into the ice cream base in two more additions.

Retrieve the loaf pan from the freezer, pour in half of the ice cream base, and scatter with half of the peanuts and half of the chocolate peanut butter cups. Top with the remaining ice cream base followed by the remaining peanuts and chocolate peanut butter cups.

Cover the pan with plastic wrap, lightly pressing down so that the plastic wrap touches the ice cream. Transfer to the freezer for at least 6 hours or preferably overnight.

When ready to serve, temper the ice cream on the counter for a few minutes to make scooping easier. Store any leftover ice cream in the loaf pan covered with plastic wrap.

Note: You can swap out the full-sized chocolate peanut butter cups with mini ones if you'd like, but I prefer the ratio of chocolate to peanut butter with the big guys.

With all my recipes, I try to strike a balance between effort and output with a max ratio of 30:70, meaning you'll put in maximum 30 percent effort for minimum 70 percent delicious payoff. For this recipe, the ratio lands somewhere around 1:99. This is probably one of the most straightforward dessert recipes I've ever written, and boy oh jeeze, is it ever delicious!

Brown Sugar Cinnamon Toast

SERVES 4

¼ cup butter, room temperature
3 tablespoons dark brown sugar, packed
½ teaspoon cinnamon
½ teaspoon kosher salt
4 thick slices Pullman loaf or challah
Vanilla ice cream, for serving

Heat a large nonstick skillet over medium heat.

In a small bowl, beat together the butter, brown sugar, cinnamon, and salt. Spread the butter mixture over both sides of the bread. Add the bread to the skillet and fry until golden and crisp, about 2 minutes per side.

Serve the warm caramelized toast with a scoop of vanilla ice cream.

Note: For a handheld treat, cut each piece of toast in half and sandwich the ice cream in the middle.

This is kind of like a chocolaty pouding chômeur, a traditional French Canadian dessert. If you ask me, it's the only instance of playing things hot and cold that actually leads to a match made in heaven.

Saucy Chocolate Fudge Cake Sundaes

SERVES 4 TO 6

FOR THE CAKE BATTER

¼ cup butter, melted
½ cup sugar
½ cup milk
1 egg
1 teaspoon vanilla extract
1 cup all-purpose flour
¼ cup cocoa powder
1½ teaspoons baking powder
½ teaspoon kosher salt

FOR THE SAUCE

¾ cup dark brown sugar, packed
¼ cup cocoa powder
1 cup hot coffee
¼ teaspoon vanilla extract
¼ teaspoon kosher salt

FOR THE SUNDAES

Vanilla ice cream
Canned whipped cream
Chopped peanuts
Maraschino cherries

Preheat your oven to 350°F and lightly grease a 9-inch square glass or ceramic casserole dish with nonstick cooking spray (see note).

For the cake batter, in a medium bowl, stir together the butter, sugar, milk, egg, and vanilla. As you want this to be fudgy and almost brownie-like, there's no need to beat or cream the wet ingredients, as that would add air to the mix and make the cake too light. Sift in the flour, cocoa powder, baking powder, and salt and stir just to combine. Transfer the batter to the prepared dish and set aside.

For the sauce, in a 2-cup glass measuring cup or a bowl with a spout, whisk the brown sugar and cocoa powder together. Pour in the hot coffee and vanilla and whisk to combine. Retrieve the dish with the cake batter and very slowly pour the hot cocoa mixture over the back of a spatula or spoon onto the top of the batter, being sure not to mix it in.

Carefully transfer the dish to the oven and bake for 18 to 20 minutes, or until the cake floats to the top and is just set, with the center still a little jiggly.

Assemble the sundaes by layering ice cream with scoops of the saucy chocolate fudge cake. Top with whipped cream, chopped peanuts, and a cherry, if you'd like.

Note: Since they are slower to heat, a glass or ceramic casserole dish ensures that the edges of the cake stay fudgy and the center stays saucy.

When Aaron and I first started dating and were in that stage when you start sharing slightly braggy stories from your past, he told me that his big claim to fame was winning the Blenheim Cherry Pit Spit competition when he was 11 years old. Did I understand what this meant? Absolutely not. But I did surmise that this stone-cold cutie *loves* cherries.

Cherry Almond Orange Crostata

MAKES ONE 10-INCH TART

- ½ cup butter, room temperature
- ½ cup sugar
- 1 teaspoon almond extract, divided
- 1 egg
- 2 egg yolks, divided
- 1½ cups all-purpose flour
- ¼ cup almond flour
- 1 teaspoon baking powder
- ¼ teaspoon kosher salt
- 1 cup pitted fresh or frozen cherries, thawed and drained if frozen
- 1 jar (8 oz) cherry jam
- 1 orange, zested
- 1 tablespoon water
- 2–3 tablespoons sliced almonds

Lightly grease a 10-inch removable-bottom tart pan or 9-inch standard pie plate with nonstick cooking spray. Place on a sheet pan and set aside.

In a large bowl, beat the butter and sugar together. Add ½ teaspoon of almond extract, the egg, and one egg yolk and beat until smooth. Stir in the flour, almond flour, baking powder, and salt. Transfer the dough to the fridge to chill for 30 minutes.

Meanwhile, if using fresh cherries, cut them in half. Add the cherries to a large bowl, along with the jam, orange zest, and remaining ½ teaspoon of almond extract. Stir gently to combine.

Transfer about two-thirds of the dough to the prepared pan and press it into the bottom and up the sides. Spread the jam mixture overtop and set aside.

On a lightly floured work surface, roll out the remaining dough to a scant ¼ inch thick. Cut the dough into 1-inch-wide strips and lay in a lattice pattern over the tart. Unlike with traditional pie dough, this pastry is quite delicate, so you will not be able to weave the lattice. Simply lay it in a grid pattern over the filling. Trim the edges and transfer to the fridge to chill for 30 minutes.

Place your oven rack in the lower third of your oven and preheat it to 350°F.

Beat the remaining egg yolk with the tablespoon of water and brush over the lattice top of the tart. Scatter with the almonds and bake for 30 to 35 minutes, or until golden brown.

Cool completely before slicing and serving. Cover and store any leftover crostata at room temperature for up to 4 days.

Note: If using frozen cherries, reserve the cherry juice for cocktails or mocktails. It's really tasty when stirred into soda water with a squiggle of orange juice.

I live with two pie aficionados. If I put anything in pastry, savory or sweet, it's going to be a hit. So to say I know my way around pies would be accurate, but there is one that has remained my proverbial white whale. Until recently, I had never successfully made a blueberry pie and had thought myself relegated to the world of blueberry crisps, cobblers, and grunts. But in classic (read: stubborn) Mary fashion, I didn't give up. Rather than continue to try for a deep-dish behemoth, I successfully switched up my tactic and turned to my personal fave pie, the galette.

Blueberry Galette

SERVES 8

FOR THE PASTRY

1 cup all-purpose flour

½ teaspoon kosher salt

½ cup cold butter, cubed

¼ cup ice water + 1 teaspoon white vinegar

FOR THE FILLING

4 cups fresh blueberries

1 lemon, zested

1 teaspoon almond extract

½ cup sugar

3 tablespoons cornstarch

¼ teaspoon ground ginger

¼ teaspoon freshly grated nutmeg

1 egg

1 tablespoon milk or water

Turbinado sugar, optional

Vanilla ice cream, for serving

For the pastry, in the bowl of your food processor, pulse the flour and salt. Add the butter and pulse into hazelnut-sized pieces (this should take only four to five pulses). Pour in the water and vinegar mixture and pulse until the mixture begins to climb up the sides of your food processor and holds together when squeezed in your hand.

Turn the dough out onto a piece of plastic wrap, then gather and press it into a 1-inch-thick disk. Refrigerate for 30 to 45 minutes to allow the flour to hydrate and re-chill the butter.

While the crust chills, make the filling. In a bowl, combine the blueberries, lemon zest, almond extract, sugar, cornstarch, ginger, and nutmeg. Set aside.

Place your oven rack in the lowest position and preheat the oven to 400°F. Line a rimmed sheet pan with parchment paper.

Once the dough is chilled, place it on a lightly floured surface. Roll it out into a ¼-inch-thick circle and transfer it to the prepared sheet pan. Spoon the fruit mixture onto the center of the dough, leaving a 2-inch border around the edge. Fold the edges of the galette up and over the fruit to form a crust.

In a small bowl, whisk the egg and milk or water, then brush the egg wash onto the crust of the galette. Sprinkle with turbinado sugar, if using, and bake for 40 to 45 minutes, or until golden and the fruit is bubbling and jammy.

Allow the galette to cool fully to room temperature before serving with a scoop of vanilla ice cream. The galette will keep covered at room temperature for up to 2 days or in the fridge for up to 5 days.

Note: After many failed attempts, I found that the key to a successful blueberry dessert is allowing it to cool completely before serving. That allows the pectin and starch in the filling to set up.

When I was growing up, my mom was never the biggest fan of cooking. She was a busy single parent running her own business, and at the end of the day, we often all loaded into the car to go to one of our favorite chain restaurants for dinner. We typically stuck to the savory side of menus, choosing chicken fajitas, burgers, pasta, or all-you-can-eat salads, but a lava cake was one restaurant dessert we could never pass up.

Chocolate Hazelnut Lava Cakes

SERVES 4

- ½ cup butter
- 4 teaspoons cocoa powder
- 3½ oz dark chocolate, finely chopped
- ½ cup sugar
- 2 eggs
- 2 egg yolks
- ¾ cup all-purpose flour
- ¼ teaspoon kosher salt
- 4 tablespoons chocolate hazelnut spread
- Vanilla ice cream, for serving

Preheat your oven to 400°F and set four 1-cup ramekins on a sheet pan.

In a small saucepan over low heat, melt the butter. Using a pastry or basting brush, grease the bottoms and sides of the ramekins with a bit of the melted butter. Add 1 teaspoon of cocoa powder to each ramekin, then tip the ramekins so that the cocoa coats the entire inside. Turn the ramekins over and tap out any excess cocoa.

Place the chocolate in a medium heatproof bowl, then turn up the heat under the butter to medium. When the butter begins to bubble, remove it from the heat and pour it over the chocolate. Set aside for 5 minutes to allow the chocolate to melt, then whisk until smooth.

Meanwhile, in a large bowl, combine the sugar, eggs, and egg yolks. Using a hand mixer, beat for 2 minutes until pale yellow and thickened. Sift in the flour and salt and gently fold to combine.

Pour the chocolate mixture into the sugar-egg mixture and fold just until combined.

Divide the batter between the ramekins and plop 1 tablespoon of chocolate hazelnut spread in the center of each. Press the chocolate hazelnut spread down into the center so that it is covered by the batter.

Bake for 10 to 12 minutes, or until the tops are matte and the edges pull away from the sides but the center is still wobbly.

Allow the cakes to cool for 1 minute, then loosen the sides of each with a butter knife and place a serving plate on top. Quickly flip the cakes over and remove the ramekins. Alternatively, you can serve these cakes in their ramekins.

Serve immediately with a scoop of ice cream.

Note: For a fully homemade treat, swap the chocolate hazelnut spread for Chocolate Pecan Butter (page 16).

Any Canadian who grew up in the '90s and went to a sleepover will recognize the late-night freezer treat that inspired this cake. There was just something so thrilling about sneaking into the deep freezer late at night, forks in hand, and digging straight into the *deep* pan of that *delicious* dessert. My personal fave was always the marble variety, and while you can always spread the frosting overtop, go for a star-tipped piping bag for pure nostalgia.

Tall 'n' Tasty Cake

MAKES ONE 9-BY-13-INCH CAKE

FOR THE CAKE

½ cup + 2 tablespoons canola oil, divided
2 cups sugar
2 eggs
1 cup buttermilk
2 teaspoons vanilla extract
2½ cups all-purpose flour
2 teaspoons baking soda
1 teaspoon baking powder
½ teaspoon kosher salt
¼ cup boiling water
3 tablespoons cocoa powder

FOR THE FROSTING

3½ oz milk chocolate, roughly chopped
¼ cup butter
½ cup sour cream
½ teaspoon vanilla extract
¼ teaspoon instant espresso powder, optional
¼ teaspoon kosher salt
1½ cups icing sugar
2 tablespoons chocolate sprinkles

For the cake, preheat your oven to 350°F and lightly grease a 9-by-13-inch baking pan with nonstick cooking spray.

In a large bowl, whisk ½ cup of oil with the sugar and eggs. Whisk in the buttermilk and vanilla and set aside.

In a separate bowl, whisk together the flour, baking soda, baking powder, and salt. Add the wet mixture to the dry and stir just until combined. Pour in the boiling water and carefully mix to combine. The mixture will be quite thin but that's OK—this addition of boiling water makes for an incredibly moist and level cake.

In a medium bowl, whisk the cocoa powder with the remaining 2 tablespoons of oil. Scoop about 2 cups of the vanilla cake batter into the cocoa mixture and whisk to combine.

Pour the remaining vanilla cake batter into the prepared pan and drizzle with the cocoa-infused batter. Using a butter knife, swirl the batters to achieve a marbled effect. Bake for 35 to 40 minutes, or until the cake is set and a toothpick inserted in the center comes out clean. Allow the cake to cool completely in the pan.

While the cake cools, make the frosting. In a medium heatproof bowl set over a pot of simmering water, melt the chocolate and butter. Remove the melted chocolate mixture from the heat and stir in the sour cream, vanilla, instant espresso powder, if using, and salt. Gradually beat in the icing sugar.

Leaving the cake in the pan, spread or pipe the frosting on the cake, then scatter with sprinkles. Serve immediately or cover the cake and store in the fridge for up to 3 days. For optimal texture, remove the cake from the fridge about 30 minutes before serving.

I haven't the foggiest where my mom picked up the idea or name for this sweet treat, but it was her go-to cake for my brother's birthday throughout his teenaged years. It was a bonkers mix of boxed devil's food cake, sweetened condensed milk, caramel sauce, and whipped cream (with very little crossover to its namesake). Here, I've snazzed it up a bit with homemade cake and caramel.

Skor Cake

MAKES ONE 9-BY-13-INCH SHEET CAKE

FOR THE CAKE

2 cups all-purpose flour
2 cups sugar
¾ cup cocoa powder
2 teaspoons baking soda
1 teaspoon baking powder
1 teaspoon kosher salt
1 cup buttermilk
½ cup canola oil
2 eggs
1 teaspoon vanilla extract
½ cup hot coffee

FOR THE TOPPINGS

½ cup sugar
1 tablespoon water
2¼ cups whipping cream, divided
3 tablespoons butter
½ teaspoon vanilla extract
Flaky salt
1 (10 fl oz) sweetened condensed milk
1 cup toffee almond bits, such as Skor bits

For the cake, preheat your oven to 350°F and lightly grease a 9-by-13-inch pan with nonstick cooking spray. Line the bottom of the pan with parchment paper and set aside.

Into a large bowl, sift the flour, sugar, cocoa powder, baking soda, baking powder, and salt.

In a large glass measuring cup, whisk together the buttermilk, oil, eggs, and vanilla. Add the wet ingredients to the dry and whisk to combine. Pour in the hot coffee and whisk just until combined.

Pour the batter into the prepared cake pan and bake for 35 to 40 minutes, or until the cake is springy and a toothpick inserted in the center comes out clean. Set aside to cool completely in the pan.

Meanwhile, for the toppings, in a small saucepan over medium heat, combine the sugar and water. Without stirring or touching the sugar, allow the mixture to melt and caramelize. This should take 5 to 7 minutes. Once the sugar starts to turn golden, gently swirl the pan to ensure that the mixture caramelizes evenly.

As soon as the mixture turns amber in color, pour in ¼ cup of cream and whisk to combine. Add the butter and continue to cook for 1 minute. Turn off the heat and carefully add the vanilla and flaky salt. Set aside to cool.

When the cake and caramel are cool, whip the remaining 2 cups of cream to medium peaks. Using the handle of a wooden spoon, poke a grid of holes into the cake. Pour in most of the caramel followed by the whole can of sweetened condensed milk. Scatter half of the almond toffee bits overtop, then top with the whipped cream. Drizzle with the remaining caramel and scatter with the remaining toffee bits.

Serve immediately or cover and keep in the fridge for up to 2 days.

Note: If caramel seems a bit daunting, just pull a Myra Berg and pick up a jar at the grocery store. You can usually find it near the ice cream cones.

When I was a kid, the only cake I wanted for my birthday was a grocery store strawberry shortcake. What I didn't realize at the time was that this store-bought impostor is not, in fact, a shortcake at all but rather a stacked vanilla cake filled to the brim with cream and the freshest December strawberries the grocery store could find!

Grocery Store Strawberry Shortcake

MAKES ONE 2-LAYER 9-INCH CAKE

FOR THE CAKE

2¾ cups all-purpose flour
¼ cup cornstarch
2 teaspoons baking powder
1 teaspoon baking soda
½ teaspoon kosher salt
1½ cups buttermilk
2 teaspoons vanilla extract
¼ teaspoon almond extract, optional
6 tablespoons butter, room temperature
1¾ cups sugar
⅓ cup canola oil
3 eggs, room temperature
2 egg yolks, room temperature

FOR THE FILLING & TOPPING

2 cups cold whipping cream
3 tablespoons instant vanilla pudding mix
2–4 tablespoons icing sugar
½ teaspoon vanilla extract
12–14 oz strawberries, sliced or quartered

For the cake, preheat your oven to 350°F and grease two 9-inch round cake pans with nonstick cooking spray. Line the bottom of each with a circle of parchment paper and set aside.

Into a medium bowl, sift the flour, cornstarch, baking powder, baking soda, and salt and set aside.

In a glass measuring cup or small bowl, combine the buttermilk, vanilla extract, and almond extract, if using, and set aside.

Using your hand mixer or stand mixer fitted with the paddle attachment, beat the butter until a little fluffy. Add the sugar, oil, eggs, and egg yolks and beat on high until the mixture is a little lighter in color and texture. Scrape down the sides of the bowl and gently mix in about one-third of the flour mixture. Stir in half of the buttermilk mixture followed by another third of the flour. Stir in the remaining buttermilk followed by the remaining flour.

Divide the batter between the prepared pans and bake for 30 minutes, or until golden brown, springy, and a skewer inserted in the center comes out clean. Allow the cakes to cool for 5 to 10 minutes in the pan before turning them out onto a wire rack to cool completely to room temperature.

When the cakes are cool, prepare the filling and topping. In a large bowl, combine the cream, instant pudding mix, icing sugar, and vanilla. Using a hand mixer, whip on medium speed to stiff peaks.

Place one cake on a serving plate or cake pedestal and top with half of the whipped cream and half of the strawberries. Gently place the second cake on top and top with the remaining whipped cream and strawberries. This cake is best served the day you make it, but leftovers can be covered and stored in the fridge for up to 4 days.

Note: Stable whipped cream is the key to this recipe and my secret ingredient is instant pudding. The proteins in the instant pudding provided by dried milk powder bind to the fat in the cream, making the bubble structure in the whipped cream more strong and stable.

Often the shape of a gold bar indicative of the finance bros of 19th-century France, who were supposedly the original indulgers, a financier is essentially a small almond cake. I've flavored this version with browned butter, lemon, and raspberries, and I've supersized it because you can never have too much of a good thing.

Raspberry Financier

MAKES ONE 9-INCH CAKE

- 1 cup unsalted butter
- ½ cup sugar
- ¼ cup dark brown sugar, packed
- ½ cup + 2 tablespoons almond flour
- ½ cup all-purpose flour
- 1½ teaspoons baking powder
- 1 teaspoon kosher salt
- ¼ teaspoon freshly grated nutmeg
- 1 lemon, zested
- ¾ teaspoon vanilla extract, divided
- ½ teaspoon almond extract
- 5 egg whites
- 6 oz raspberries
- 1¼–1½ cups icing sugar
- 2 tablespoons milk, plus more if needed

Place the butter in a saucepan or medium skillet and set over medium heat. Allow the butter to melt, foam up, and brown, stirring occasionally. This should take 5 to 7 minutes, but keep an eye on it as it can go from browned to burnt in a flash. With a heat-resistant glass measuring cup, measure out ¾ cup of the browned butter and set the rest aside in a medium bowl.

Meanwhile, in a separate medium bowl, combine the sugar, brown sugar, almond flour, all-purpose flour, baking powder, salt, nutmeg, and lemon zest. Add the ¾ cup of browned butter to the dry mixture and beat to combine. Set the batter aside for about 5 minutes to cool slightly, then mix in ½ teaspoon of vanilla extract, the almond extract, and egg whites. Cover the bowl with plastic wrap and place in the fridge to chill for 1 hour.

When ready to bake, preheat your oven to 350°F and lightly grease a 9-inch round cake pan with nonstick cooking spray. Pour the batter into the pan and scatter with the raspberries, pressing them into the batter so that they are about half submerged.

Bake the cake for 30 to 35 minutes, or until golden, springy, and a toothpick inserted in the center of the cake comes out clean. Allow the cake to cool in the pan for 15 minutes.

Meanwhile, prepare the glaze by adding 1¼ cups of icing sugar to the remaining browned butter. If the browned butter has firmed up, first gently heat it over low or in the microwave to melt. Add the milk and remaining ¼ teaspoon of vanilla and whisk to combine. If the glaze is a little thin, add more icing sugar. If it's a little thick, add a splash more milk.

Turn the cake out onto a wire rack and arrange domed side up. Pour the glaze over the warm cake and serve immediately, or allow the cake to cool and the glaze to set. Store the cake covered at room temperature for up to 5 days.

Thank you!

First off, how lucky am I to have someone like you reading this book and cooking my recipes! Thank you for inviting me into your home through my books and TV shows, and for being as excited as I am about food. Hearing from you, meeting you, and getting to see how the recipes I write become some of your family favorites is one of the truest pleasures in my life. It fills my heart to hear that you've found joy in the kitchen, cooking and sharing food with the people you love. Getting to be a small part of that is, quite simply, a thrill.

To my outstanding team at Appetite by Random House, thank you for your unending support and expertise and for being as amped as I am about food and all things delicious. Robert McCullough, from the first moment we met, I knew I had found a kindred spirit. You are a champion for authors, an excellent dinner date, and a wonderful friend. Thank you for it all. Zoe Maslow! Editor extraordinaire! Thank you for always seeing the vision, for picking up my random phone calls, and for making me feel like I know what I'm doing. To Jen Griffiths and Sid Watson, thank you for lending your brilliant design eyes to this book. Your ability to take my written recipes and create something as beautiful as this is wizardry at its finest. And, while you've yet to work on this book as of me writing this, a massive thank you goes out to Megan Konzelman for her energy, organizational skills, and overall wonderfulness when promoting my books. Working with you on *In Mary's Kitchen* was a delight and I can't wait to get started on this one.

Without Kyla, Michelle, and Cailen, this book would be nothing more than typed words on a page. Kyla, holy absolute Toledo, what a wonder you are! Your ability to capture my recipes in a more flattering light than I ever thought possible was truly something to behold. Thank you for your eye, for your energy, and for making this book such a joy to shoot. And it's true, I *don't* know your husband, Brenda. Michelle! What would I have done without you? Prior to this book, I have always worked as a bit of an island in terms of cookbook food styling but when you came ashore, it was like the sun came out. Thank you so much for lending your expert food styling to these pages and for being such a wonderful human. To my tchotchke-loving pal who I've worked with on TV shows for years, the one and only Cailen! Thank you for always understanding the brief and for bringing color and a little bit of kitsch to every setup.

And a special shout out goes to Ebti and Megan. Thank you for assisting throughout the shoot, for your skills, and for taking home leftovers at the end of the day (the real MVP move!).

To everyone who works on *The Good Stuff*, from the crew and producers to the experts and editors: thank you, thank you, thank you for the care and extremely hard work you put into each show. It is simply amazing what you all accomplish every single day, and getting to be a part of that continues to be an absolute delight.

I have had the extreme pleasure of working with some of the most amazing humans on each and every set I've been on. There are literally hundreds of people I could name here but, to keep within my page count, I'll just say thank you to everyone who shows kindness on a stressful set, who listens and answers questions, who lends their talent and skill, and who works as a team to make one nice thing. The joy and the success of anything I've ever worked on is because of the team.

Allison, I don't think I'd ever be able to put into words all that you've taught me and how grateful I am for you. You are a true leader, one of the most thoughtful, brilliant, and kind people I know, and I simply adore you. Thank you for everything.

Richelle, thank you to the moon and back for being the world's best person/human external hard drive. On the days where I'm suffering from a severe case of donkey brains, you hold it all together without missing a beat. You are a wonder and a delight, and I'm chuffed to call you a friend.

It's so special to have those friends who, no matter your mood, when you last washed your hair, or whether plans have even been made, you can always count on for the best hang. For me, that's Jenna, Kyle, and Renée. Thank you for drop-ins, dinners, nights on the back deck, and for sharing my love of starting eighteen stories in a night and only *maybe* finishing three. Renée, you make the best salads, Kyle, A+ grilling, my dude, and Jenna, your snack/dessert game is unmatched.

To my skramps, Odie, Sarah, Ali, and Simon, thank you for being such fierce friends and for your always sound and often unhinged guidance in the group chat. Thank you for potato parties, Skrampmas, and "lasagna fingers" (a.k.a. leftover lasagna cut into strips and eaten while standing in the kitchen. Simon, you are a comfort food genius).

Nikki, you are the human embodiment of joy. Seeing you move through the world bringing light to so many people is a marvel. Thank you for sharing that joy with me every single day. See you in the car—Milhouse.

Thank you to Marisa for being the most supportive best friend I could ever hope for. Even though distance, bananas bonkers schedules, and my general inability to text often keep us apart, I can't wait to be old ladies still staying up late scream-talking until we both lose our voices.

To Myra, there is a reason not a day goes by where someone doesn't tell me how much they love you. Thank you for your constant encouragement and support, for your incredible sense of humor, for emergency back pats, and for being just the best dang mom I could ever imagine! I love you!

And finally, thank you to the guy who somehow knows how to make every single day better than the last. My eyes are getting all sting-y writing this, which typically happens when my emotions override my ability to speak or, I guess in this case, write. You're sitting behind me in our home reading a book right now and I can honestly say that every moment with you, Aaron, even the most mundane, is my best moment.

Index

C